ARISTOPHANES

in an hour

BY CARL R. MUELLER

D1215802

SUSAN C. MOORE, SERIES EDITOR

PLAYWRIGHTS in an hour
know the playwright, love the play

IN AN HOUR BOOKS • HANOVER, NEW HAMPSHIRE • INANHOURBOOKS.COM
AN IMPRINT OF SMITH AND KRAUS PUBLISHERS, INC • SMITHANDKRAUS.COM

With grateful thanks to Carl R. Mueller, whose fascinating introductions to his translations of the Greek and German playwrights provided inspiration for this series.

Published by In an Hour Books
an imprint of Smith and Kraus Publishers, Inc.
177 Lyme Road, Hanover, NH 03755
inanhourbooks.com SmithandKraus.com

Know the playwright, love the play.

In an Hour, In a Minute, and Theater IQ are registered trademarks
of In an Hour Books.

Front cover design by Dan Mehling, dmehling@gmail.com
Text design by Kate Mueller, Electric Dragon Productions
Book production by Dede Cummings Design, DCDesign@sover.net

ISBN-13: 978-1-936232-07-9
ISBN-10: 1-936232-07-3
Library of Congress PCN: 2009943207

CONTENTS

Why Playwrights in an Hour?

This new series by Smith and Kraus Publishers titled Playwrights in an Hour has a dual purpose for being: one academic, the other general. For the general reader, this volume, as well as the many others in the series, offers in compact form the information needed for a basic understanding and appreciation of the works of each volume's featured playwright. Which is not to say that there don't exist volumes on end devoted to each playwright under consideration. But inasmuch as few are blessed with enough time to read the splendid scholarship that is available, a brief, highly focused accounting of the playwright's life and work is in order. The central feature of the series, a thirty- to forty-page essay, integrates the playwright into the context of his or her time and place. The volumes, though written to high standards of academic integrity, are accessible in style and approach to the general reader as well as to the student and, of course, to the theater professional and theatergoer. These books will serve for the brushing up of one's knowledge of a playwright's career, to the benefit of theater work or theatergoing. The Playwrights in an Hour series represents all periods of Western theater: Aeschylus to Shakespeare to Wedekind to Ibsen to Williams to Beckett, and on to the great contemporary playwrights who continue to offer joy and enlightenment to a grateful world.

Carl R. Mueller
School of Theater, Film and Television
Department of Theater
University of California, Los Angeles

Introduction

Aristophanes, who lived between the last half of the fifth century BCE and the first part of the fourth century BCE is the oldest comic dramatist known to history. He is also one of the very best. Writing for a theater dominated by such heroic playwrights as Aeschylus, Sophocles, and Euripides, Aristophanes was absolutely relentless in satirizing their tragic subjects and their tragic forms, and absolutely fearless in lampooning many of the most respected religious, political, philosophical, and artistic figures of his day.

Though Aristophanes was a passionate pacifist, he was far from a radical firebrand. Rather, he was essentially a conservative thinker. True, he nagged at warmongers such as King Cleon for preventing an honorable peace with Sparta (Cleon questioned the patriotism of anyone who suggested a negotiated peace). But Aristophanes also took aim at such liberal sophists as Socrates for his Cloudcuckooland thinking, and Euripides for his presumed misogyny. Nor was Aristophanes very tolerant toward contemporary gay relationships.

But the issue that most powerfully motivated Aristophanes was the endless Peloponnesian Wars, and a large part of his writing consisted of fantastic fantasies about how to the end the hostilities. In this regard, his plays often had the quality of wishful dreams. In *Peace*, for instance, the play ends with a nude courtesan, Peace, being pulled out of a pi, and paraded around the city. For Aristophanes, eroticism represents the very opposite of war. The same kind of daydream animates *Lysistrata*, where a passionate housewife persuades the women of Athens and Sparta to withhold erotic favors from their husbands until the men agree to end the war. It is significant that all of Aristophanes' male characters sport enormous erect penises known as the phallos. In *Lysistrata*, for obvious reasons, deprivation makes their erections particularly large. In a production of the play performed at the American Repertory Theatre in 2001, the phalluses were represented as colored balloons. At the end of the show, following an outbreak of peace, the women took their needles and burst them.

Much of Aristophanes' comedy is based on the contradiction between high spiritual aspirations and low physical functions. Indeed, this kind of Functional Comedy would later become the basis for much Western burlesque and farce. I'm not referring to the witty, often incorporeal banter between men and women in the act of courtship, but rather the more raunchy, raucous comedy found in the low characters of Shakespeare. In the first part of the twentieth century in America, Minsky burlesques — named after the Minsky brothers — embodied a similar outlaw tradition. First Bananas like Bert Lahr and Bobby Clark rarely performed an erotic skit without the aid of a well-endowed showgirl as a nubile comic butt. ("Nursey, nursey, what are you busting in here like that?" asks the Doctor Kronkite–type character in playwright Neil Simon's *The Sunshine Boys*.)

The great hidden subject of comedy, as Aristophanes was the first to demonstrate, is the conflict between Eros and Thanatos, or Desire and Death. This is why war was such anathema to this great comic playwright and why carnal relations remained his greatest hope for the perpetuation of human life.

Robert Brustein
Founding Director of the Yale and American Repertory Theatres,
Distinguished Scholar in Residence, Suffolk University
Senior Research Fellow, Harvard University

Aristophanes

IN A MINUTE

AGE	YEAR (BCE)	
—	450	Enter Aristophanes (born about 450, exact birth date unknown).
1	449	Persians defeated by Greeks at Salamis.
2	448	The Acropolis is rebuilt in Athens.
3	447	The Wall of Jerusalem built by Nehemiah and Ezra.
7	443	Periclean Age: Pericles elected Athenian general.
11	439	Plebeian revolt in Rome.
13	437	Athenians colonize the North Aegean coast.
19	431	Peloponnesian War between Athens and Sparta.
20	430	Devastating plague in Athens.
21	429	Sophocles — *Oedipus the King*
23	**427**	**Aristophanes — *Banqueters***
24	**426**	**Aristophanes — *Babylonians***
25	**425**	**Aristophanes — *Acharnians* wins first prize at Athens in new category, comedy.**
26	424	Xerxes II becomes king of Persia.
28	**422**	**Aristophanes — *Wasps* (not about White Anglo Saxon Protestants)**
29	421	Greece and Sparta sign short-lived peace of Nicias.
30	420	Euripides — *Electra*
32	**ca. 418**	**Aristophanes — *Clouds II***
35	415	Athens invades Sicily and Syracuse.
36	**414**	**Aristophanes — *Birds* wins second prize at Athens.**
39	411	"Oligarchs" overthrow Athenian democracy.
41	409	Sophocles — *Philoctetes* wins first prize at Athens.
42	408	Euripides — *Orestes*
44	406	Exit Sophocles and Euripides.
45	**405**	**Aristophanes — *Frogs***
46	404	Peloponnesian War ends.
47	403	Democracy is restored in Athens.
51	399	Socrates tried and executed in Athens.
54	396	Plato — *The Apology*
64	**386**	**Exit Aristophanes (died about 386–385).**

In one minute or less, this section gives you a snapshot of the playwright's world. From historical events to the literary landscape of the time, this brief list catalogues events that directly or indirectly impacted the playwright's writing.

Aristophanes

HIS WORKS

[Wrote 44 plays. All Caps = existing plays]

DRAMATIC WORKS

ACHARNIANS

Aeolosicon I

Aeolosicon II

Amphiaraus

Anagyrus

Babylonians

Banqueters

BIRDS

Clouds I

CLOUDS II

Cocolus

Daidalus

Danaids

Dionysos Shipwrecked

Drama I or Centaur

Drama II or Niobus

Farmers

FROGS

Fry Cooks

Gerytades

Heroes

Islands

This section presents a complete list of the playwright's works.

Onstage with Aristophanes

*Introducing Colleagues and
Contemporaries of Aristophanes*

THEATER

Crates, Athenian Old Comedy playwright [mid-5th c.]
Cratinus, Athenian Old Comedy playwright [520–423]
Euripides, Athenian tragic playwright [ca. 480–406]
Sophocles, Athenian tragic playwright [496–406]
Sophron, Syracusan writer of mimes [ca. 5th c.]

ARTS

Micon, Greek painter [mid-5th c.]
Phidias, Greek sculptor [ca. 480–ca. 430]
Polyclitus, Greek sculptor [450–420]
Polygnotus, Greek painter [500–440]
Praxiteles, Greek sculptor [ca. 4th c.]

POLITICS/MILITARY

Agesilaus II, king of Sparta [444–360]
Alcibiades, Athenian general and politician [ca. 450–404]
Artaxerxes, king of Persia [ca. 5th c.]
Cyrus the Younger, Persian prince and general [ca. 5th c.]
Darius II, king of Persia [ca. 5th c.–404]
Herodotus, Greek historian [ca. 484–ca. 425]
Nicias, Athenian statesman and general [469–413]
Pericles, Athenian statesman and general [ca. 495–429]
Thucydides, Greek historian [ca. 460–ca. 395]
Xenophon, Athenian soldier, [ca. 430–354]
Xerxes II, Persian king [ca. 5th c.]

This section lists contemporaries whom the playwright may or may not have known. Since fewer notables are known from the Classical Period, we have included some who predated the playwright.

SCIENCE

Callicrates, designed rebuilding of the Athenian Acropolis
[mid-5th c.]

Hippocrates, Greek physician [ca. 460–ca. 370]

Ictinus, designed rebuilding of the Athenian Acropolis [mid-5th c.]

Praxagoras, Greek physician [ca. 4th c.]

Protagoras, Greek mathematician and philosopher [ca. 490–420]

RELIGION/PHILOSOPHY

Anaxagoras, Greek philosopher from Asia Minor [ca. 500–428]

Democritus, Greek philosopher [ca. 460–ca. 370]

Empedocles, Greek philosopher [ca. 490–430]

Ezra, Hebrew scribe [ca. 5th c.]

Meh-Ti, Chinese philosopher [ca. 5th c.]

Mo-tzu, Chinese philosopher [ca. 470–391]

Plato, Greek philosopher [428–348]

Socrates, Greek philosopher [470–399]

LITERATURE

Pindar, Greek composer and poet [522–443]

ARISTOPHANES

in an hour

BEGINNINGS

Of the many tragic playwrights practicing in Athens during the fifth century BCE, the work of only three remains. Of the many comic playwrights writing in Athens during the same period, the work of only one has not been lost. Why, then, should the work of only four of these luminaries have survived? One answer might be that they represented the cream of the crop. Their plays were popular and received numerous other productions after their first appearance in competition in Athens. They were then produced not only in outlying regions away from Athens but as far away as Sicily and the Athenian colonies that dotted the coast of Asia Minor. This may have helped preserve them. We are left with the big three of Athenian fifth-century tragedy: Aeschylus, Sophocles, and Euripides — and with Aristophanes.

THE THEATER AND ITS FORM

What was the Athenian theater of the fifth century BCE like? Imagine the theater at Epidaurus, perhaps the best-known example. Though it

---

This is the core of the book. The essay places the playwright in the context of his world and analyzes the influences and inspirations within that world.

was built 150 years after Aristophanes was writing, it gives us the basic idea. Furthest from the audience was a building with three doors out of which actors could emerge. On top of the building was a crane with which gods could be flown in or flown out at critical stages of the play, when a *deus ex machina* was called for. In front of the building were a number of columns, and even nearer the audience a raised terrace or stage area where the action took place. In front of all that was a striking element, the orchestra, a perfectly round and very large circle made of pounded earth or finished in stone. In it, the chorus performed. All these were viewed from the round circular seats for the masses of people that came, and the numbers were very large. Up to 20,000, maybe even 30,000, people viewed the plays of Aristophanes and others.

COSTUMES

The costuming of Attic tragedy was grand and richly outfitted. In comedy, however, costumes reflected the everyday clothing of the audience. Kings, queens, ambassadors, and potentates in the courts dressed for the occasion, but sausage sellers, informers, slaves, farmers and their families, and juvenile delinquents were dressed like themselves, and it is these people that Aristophanes' plays are largely about. Yet Old Comedy costumes were frequently grotesque to emphasize various parts of the anatomy: stomachs, buttocks, and so forth. And let us not overlook the phallus that almost certainly all the male characters sported. The phallus was one of considerable dimension, as we learn from much painted Greek pottery and statuettes of the time. Worn in full display, and unselfconsciously, outside the costume, it was made of leather. It could be either flaccid (though still large), or erect.

MASKS

The size of the Athenian theater required very good voice projection. Some speculate that masks were used as a kind of megaphone to project voices to the furthest rows. There is also evidence that masks were a carryover from cult ceremonies. Also, adolescent rites of passage were known from Sparta. Greek masks probably originated, however, from the rites of Dionysus. A very practical reason for the use of masks was the limited number of actors on the Greek stage. There were usually three or four actors in tragedies, and perhaps four for comedies. Masks allowed a limited number of actors to play multiple characters.

One must also not forget that masks were helpful in disguising the male actor, who traditionally assumed female roles. Women were excluded from theatrical performance. As for the numbers of non-speaking actors on stage, there was no limit. Exciting stage effects with scores of extras would not have been unusual.

ACTING

Unfortunately, little is known regarding the style of acting seen on the Athenian stage, whether for tragedy or comedy. With an audience numbering twenty thousand, the style cannot have been subtle. And it's important to remember that all performers were wearing masks. With facial expressions lacking, there must have been considerable use of body language employing torso and arms.

The plays themselves tell us the various modes of delivery that were required of an actor. Song and dance were everywhere in Greek theater, whether tragedy or comedy. Much of it, though not all, was from the chorus. Speech was exchanged between the play's characters and the leader of the chorus. There was also an intermediate sort of speech that can be called *chant* that was exchanged both within the chorus and between the characters. Each of these modes of communication, with few exceptions, was in verse. The "speech mode" was in iambic trimeter, closer than the others to normal speech.

CHORUS

The importance of the chorus cannot be overestimated. Even before tragedy, in Athens especially, there was a long tradition of dithyramb choruses competing in both song and dance. In the days of tragedy, there were separate competitions devoted to the dithyramb. In Aeschylus' day the tragic chorus was made up of twelve men, then Sophocles added three more, for a total of fifteen. In his *Tragedy in Athens* David Wiles gives a brilliant and convincing exposition of the degree to which the tragic chorus participated in the theatrical event. He posits (with help from other scholars) that choreographed movements of the chorus were quite active. Previously it had been thought that the chorus moved in straight lines in highly formalized ways. This new insight allows us to find many examples of highly active choruses. In comedy the chorus numbered twenty-four as opposed to tragedy's fifteen. And when choruses of twenty-four members actively occupied the Greek theater orchestra, as in most productions, they were intricately choreographed. It must have been a major sight to behold.

In tragedy the Chorus generally represents a defined group of individuals: a Chorus of Furies, Sailors, or Theban Women. In Old Comedy, though there are choruses of humans — Knights, Acharnians, Phoenician Women. A good number of Aristophanes' plays, existing as well as lost, have choruses that are nonhuman: Wasps, Birds, Frogs, Storks. Then there is the Chorus of Clouds. Most frequently, too, it is the Chorus that gives the play its name.

One of the most important functions of the Chorus in Aristophanes is associated with a structural part of the play known as the *parabasis*. In the *parabasis*, the Chorus addresses the audience directly. In some of the *parabases*, the Chorus maintains its assigned dramatic role (as knights, clouds, Acharnians). In others the Chorus drops its role and speaks directly for the playwright. "Our playwright thinks . . ." such and such of this and that matter. Dramatic illusion is, of course, maintained (at least for the most part) in the first instance. It is broken entirely in the second. As Kenneth Dover indicates, the initial entry of the Chorus may at times precipitate a moment of violence, or near-violence, as in *Birds* or *Acharnians*. They are often hostile to the play's hero and need to be won over, after which they are on his side and give him all the support he needs.

MUSIC

Of music in Archaic and Classical Greece we know very little. Some music scores survive, but they are largely fragmentary and date from the Hellenistic period or later. The Greeks were knowledgeable about a great many musical instruments, especially from their eastern neighbors. They adopted only two main sorts: a stringed instrument (lyre) and a wind instrument or pipe (*aulos*). The *aulos* was not a flute but was sounded with a reed (single and double). In tragedy as well as comedy in the fifth century, the double-pipe *aulos* was the instrument of choice to accompany the musical sections of the dramatic action.

The musical element in the performance of fifth-century tragedy was of primary importance. It is of no less importance in Old Comedy. There were a number of choral sections that cover generally short passages of time. During this time, the singing and dancing Chorus holds the center of attention in the orchestra. In addition, there are sections in which song is exchanged between characters. There is also an alternation between spoken dialogue and recitative or song. The latter was often between a character or characters and the Chorus.

THE ORIGINS OF OLD COMEDY

Of the origins of Attic Old Comedy we know next to nothing with any certainty. As early as the mid-fourth century, Aristotle presents the earliest theory regarding its genesis. According to him, comedy developed out of the improvisations, or *komos,* by leaders of ancient phallic fertility ceremonies and the reciters of phallic songs. Their function was to suggest to the gods that the tribe and the earth be made fertile. Or, if that were already the situation, to thank them for the gift received. According to Aristotle, such fertility ceremonies were still current in many cities and towns of his time.

A more current hypothesis of Old Comedy's origin is put forward by Dover. "In many preliterate cultures," he notes, "there are public occasions on which people pretend humorously to be somebody other than themselves, and it is a safe assumption that comedy, so defined, was of great antiquity among the Greeks (possibly of incomparably greater antiquity than tragedy)." He continues by saying that the word *komodoi* means *komos*-singers, and that a *komos* "is a company of men behaving and singing in a happy and festive manner." In Athens from the fourth century there is a series of inscriptions that lists all the winners in the City Dionysia from the beginning. In each case the order of entrants is as follows: boys' chorus, men's chorus, comedy, and tragedy. "It appears from these data," concludes Dover, "that, so far as was known in the fourth century, a humorous adult male chorus was an archaic feature of the City Dionysia, and it is probable that comedy was a specialized development from this." Dover ends with the statement that the poet Archilocus in the seventh century and Hippomax at the close of the sixth century wrote many poems. These contain unrestrained vilification and the grossest sexual humor. "These elements in Attic Comedy," he then concludes, "thus have a distinguished literary ancestry, and it is not necessary to account for them by reference to Dionysiac ritual of any kind."

OLD COMEDY AND THE FANTASTICAL

Old Comedy and the fantastical are willing and able partners. Time seems unimportant to them, as does space. In Old Comedy a scene can be changed in the blink of an eye with no break in the action. Socrates' Blabatory in *Clouds II* is onstage along with the house of Strepsiades. Indeed, given the stage that Aristophanes had to work with, with its three doors, one of those doors is the Blabatory, the other Strepsiades' house at the other end of town. Leaving the Blabatory door, Strepsiades has only to walk to his own door and the action has shifted to another site and scene. It is a device used widely in the European theater of the Middle Ages. And it is much utilized in the Epic Theater of Brecht.

Fantastical, too, is the plot of an Aristophanes play. As Dover describes it:

> The context of the plot is the contemporary situation. In this situation, a character takes some action which may violate the laws of nature (e.g. in Aristophanes' *Peace* Trygaeus flies to the home of the gods on a giant beetle in order to release the goddess Peace from imprisonment and bring her back to earth) or may show a complete disregard for practical objections (e.g. in Aristophanes' *Acharnians* Dicaeopolis makes a private peace treaty with his country's enemies and enjoys the benefits of peace).

The most endearing things about the events of Old Comedy are "the realization of common fantasies; they involve supernatural beings of all kinds and the talking animals familiar in folklore."

SEX AND THE CITY

There seems to have been nothing under the sun regarding sex, smut, and scatology that the writers of Old Comedy in fifth century Athens felt could not serve their purpose. That purpose was to make their audience laugh. The freedom of expression traditionally inherent in Old Comedy was not found throughout Classical Athenian society. In fact, this freedom can be found, in addition to Old Comedy, only in iambic poetry.

Needless to say, not all the sex in Aristophanes is salacious. It is also a joyous expression of free and uninhibited pleasure. In *Acharnians*, Dikaiopolis, a simple farmer, is celebrating in his country district the Rural Dionysia. This festival includes the worship of Phales, the personification of the penis. Dikaiopolis sings, with gusto and a gleam of mischief in his eyes, a song in praise of the pleasures of peace:

Phales, friend of Bakkhos, god
of pretty boys with prickly cocks,
of buff and hearty naked jocks
ever prone to spring a rod!

Phales god of pretty maids
all in a row, snatch at the ready,
never doubting a firm and steady
thrust to power a well-aimed blade!

After six years, great fornicator
of girly twat and bouncing boy buns,
grand licker of holes, fond masturbator,
you're back in town with all the fun

you stole away when War came calling,
bringing us want and treaty-stalling,
deception and nefarious stonewalling,
and deprivation that we found most galling!

But here again, at my own doing,
Peace has raised her lovely head,
if only for me and my dear ones, cooing
like birds in a nest and better than dead.

But now again, Great God of the Fuck,
God of the Prick, and Lord of the Latch,
we'll raise a mighty shout, and with Luck
on our side we'll open each horny hatch,

each sweet and fluffy virgin snatch,
and play fond host to snug-holed boys
with bottoms pulsing for heavenly joys,
eager for any welcoming scratch!

And then in the dawn
we'll lie on the lawn,
beyond War's recall,
our shields on the wall!

THE FESTIVALS

The Athenian yearly calendar was filled with festivals of one sort or another, but there are two festivals in particular that are of interest to the theater historian: the Great, or City, Dionysia and the Lenaea. What singles them out is the fact that they are the only ones at which theater was produced. And because theater is at their center, these theatrical festivals are basically civic affairs and the showcases of Athenian democracy. But of the two, the City Dionysia is the most significant inasmuch as it was available to the entire Greek world. Being scheduled at the start of spring, in late March, outlying parts of the Athenian Empire could attend because the sea routes were open. On the other hand, the Lenaea was held in January, when the sea routes were inhospitable and dangerous, and so it was attended mostly by Athenian citizens.

But tragedy was not the sole reason for these festivals. They also scheduled processions, sacrifices in the theater, libations, the parade of war orphans, and the performance of dithyramb and comedy. And as summary, the final day was devoted to a review of the conduct of the festival and to the awarding of prizes.

Three tragedians competed with three plays each, plus a satyr play. They were chosen by the archon, a state official. The archon also appointed the three *chorêgoi*, who undertook the expense of equipping and training the choruses, the actors, and playwrights being paid for by the state. One judge from each of the ten tribes, or demes, of Athens was chosen to determine the winners of the competition. The winning playwright was crowned with a wreath of ivy in the theater.

As for comedy, Attic Old Comedy was institutionalized in the City Dionysia in 487. Prior to that period, according to Aristotle in his *Poetics*, comic performances were in the hands of volunteers. The arrangement of performances at the City Dionysia called for three days of theatrical performances. Each day began with three tragedies by a single playwright. This was followed by a satyr play (a comic send-up of the subject of the trilogy) by the same author. Then, single comedy by a comic playwright was performed. Aristophanes, in *Birds*, gives fair indication that this was the accepted arrangement when the birds speak at length on the virtue of having wings.

> Face it, gentlemen, what could be more practical — not to say more agreeable — than sprouting a pair of wings? Let's say one of you out there is winged, and your belly starts in to growling, you're famished, and what's more you're bored to distraction with the tragedy droning on. What do you do? Well, what you do is fly off home, scoff down a bite of lunch and, when your gut's been appeased, wing your way on back to catch the comedy. Or suppose Patrokleidês I see sitting out there feels the need to take a crap. What does *he* do? Soil his drawers? No. He flies off, dumps a load, blows a fart, catches his breath and flies on back. Or if you happen to be hanky-pankying with some councilor's wife, and you see him in the front row wedged into his official seat, off you sail to your lady's bed, sock it to her, and be back before the play's even over. And there you have it! There's nothing, nothing, can beat a pair of wings! No price too great!

AUDIENCE

The Theater of Dionysus, in which both of the theatrical festivals were held, seated perhaps twenty thousand people. It was chosen as the site of these two festivals — the City Dionysia in particular because of its international nature — in order to demonstrate on a vast scale the democratic ethos of Athens. Everyone was welcome. Alongside Athenian citizens, according to Henderson, "sat as many of those people who were otherwise debarred from civic assemblies as could get seats: women, children, even slaves, . . . and visiting foreigners. . . . "

COMEDY AND ITS FUNCTIONS

The classical Greeks, as Werner Jaeger reminds us in his *Paideia*, regarded Attic Old Comedy as "the mirror of life." Comedy, more than any other of the arts, is "tied to the realities of its time and place." And it is comedy's function to engage itself fully with those aspects of human behavior that the higher, nobler arts, like tragedy and the epic, overlook. It was in the fourth century that Aristotle, in Jaeger's words, "defined tragedy and comedy as fundamentally opposite and complementary expressions of the same primitive human instinct for imitation." Tragedy is the expression of the human need of noble minds to "imitate great men, notable deeds, and famous lives." Comedy, on the other hand, Aristotle defined as the imitative urge of the ordinary man, "with his realistic and critical outlook — to ape bad, blameworthy, and contemptible things."

In Homer there are times when the gods are described as laughing at events that pass the test of popular comedy. These events, as Jaeger has it, cater "to the instincts of the mob." And if the gods of Olympus could laugh, and at times even allow themselves to be laughed at, then humans could be laughed at too. What was there to prevent the Greek from feeling that "every human being . . . had not only the power of feeling heroic emotion and serious dignity, but the ability and the need to laugh." Aristotle defined man as "the only animal capable of laughter, though he was usually described as a thinking animal; thereby they placed laughter on the same plane with thought and speech, as an expression of intellectual freedom."

THE NATURE OF ARISTOPHANIC COMEDY

In assessing the particular nature of Aristophanes' comedy, Dover praises him for "his keen eye and ear for the absurd and the pompous."

Dover notes that his favored weapons are "parody, satire, and exaggeration to the point of fantasy." As for his favorite targets, they are political bigwigs, poets of his time, musicians, scientists, philosophers. His targets are "manifestations of cultural change in general. His sympathetic characters commonly express the feelings of men who like to be left alone to enjoy traditional pleasures in traditional ways."

No one, no class, age, or profession is safe from Aristophanes' satire. Neither is society as a whole safe from satire. Dover notes "the citizen-body as a whole, and if we interpret his plays as moral or social lessons we never find the lesson free of qualifications and complications." In *Knights*, for example, the Athenian demagogue Cleon (a favorite target for Aristophanes' satire) is "worsted not by an upright and dignified man but by an illiterate and brazen cynic, the Sausage Seller, who beats him at his own game." As for Lysistrata and her campaign against the war-making male society of her time, she is a heroine for whom the modern consciousness has nothing but praise and sympathy. And yet, Dover remarks, Aristophanes and his audience might well have viewed much of what she did as "preposterous." Not that they didn't find it funny. After all, comedy, then as now, depends largely on doing the exact opposite of what is expected, of what is normal everyday routine. It is the discrepancy with reality that makes it laughable. Given the position of women in classical Athens, Lysistrata's actions must have been, as we say, a laugh riot.

A QUESTION OF INFLUENCE

What was the effect on society at large of Aristophanes' satire? To be sure, he aggressively fought for and succeeded in raising the intellectual and artistic standards of Old Comedy. He worked on this from the time he began writing comedy in 427, four years into the Peloponnesian War. But as to his influence on society and its state of mind, it was minimal to say the least. Because of the satire leveled against Socrates in *Clouds II*, for example, Aristophanes was blamed by Plato for assisting in creating mistrust of Socrates. As to *Acharnians* and *Lysistrata*, neither managed to convince the Athenians to negotiate with Sparta for peace. And as for *Peace*, "it did not mold public opinion, but fell into line with it." And yet, says Dover, "The fact that Aristophanes survived not only Cleon's attacks, but also (with other comic poets) two oligarchic revolutions . . . and two democratic restorations should not be forgotten." And finally, Cleon, the target of Aristophanes' blistering satire, "was elected to a generalship . . . ."

EARLY PLAYS: BANQUETERS AND BABYLONIANS

Of Aristophanes' first two plays, *Banqueters* (427) and *Babylonians* (426) we do not have texts, except for very brief passages and single lines. In the case of *Banqueters*, there is an actual mention of it in the text of the revised version of *Clouds II*. The Chorus Leader addresses the audience:

> I recall in this very theater the production of my first youthful comedy, *Banqueters*, a work very highly spoken of by certain gentlemen it is my pleasure even to mention. I was, of course, at the time, a virgin playwright, a maiden so to say, unwed, too young to bear children and present them in public, and so I exposed the babe I had borne and another picked it up, to sponsor, and for you to take to your heart and nurture and educate, *you*, who are on my side and have sworn numerous pledges of your esteem for me.

What he means, of course, is that he felt that his youth precluded his producing his own play. As it happened, Callistratus undertook to produce it. In any case, the youthful Aristophanes made his debut at, possibly, the Lenaea Festival. He was seen to have been from the first, as Jaeger points out, "a critic not only of politics but of culture." *Banqueters* concerns itself with the conflict between ideals in education, old and new. This was a theme he would return to some nine or so years later in *Clouds II*. It was a fairly common theme among other contemporary Attic comic playwrights. For all of his theatrical audacity and ribaldry — indeed, obscenity — Aristophanes was basically a conservative. "Here," writes Jaeger, "he attacks the new ideal on what might seem to be a fairly inessential point — the eccentric and ill-bred conduct of its representatives.

When eventually Aristophanes returns to the topic, in *Clouds II*, almost a decade later, he has consolidated his hatred for progressive education and for the "new intellectual movement" in general. And he does so with concentrated vehemence. He has also the good fortune to find in his contemporary Socrates the perfect carrier of the intellectual, sophistic pose that he so distrusted: Socrates, whom "nature herself in a fit of humor had made . . . a perfect comic mask, in the shape of a Silenus-face with a snub nose, protruding lips, and goggling eyes." To be sure, Aristophanes' Socrates is not the profound moral leader and thinker that he is in Plato. That side was not to be denied, but it was quite unusable in comedy. It is said that even Socrates enjoyed the outrageous liberties taken by the playwright. Needless to say, comedy at its best thrives on bending reality to serve its comedic purpose.

Of *Babylonians* we know even less than we know about *Banqueters*. It was Aristophanes' second play, produced in 426 at the City Dionysia. It may have won first prize in the comedy competition. We also know that Dionysus appeared in the play. This was the same Dionysus who was later to appear in *Frogs*. What he does in *Babylonians*, however, except go to a trial, is not known. The one thing we do know is that the play apparently severely criticized the foreign policy of the contemporary demagogue Cleon. Dikaiopolis, the comic hero of *Acharnians* the following year, addresses the audience on the subject in place of the author:

> Aha, and then there's Kleon! And do I know Kleon! That little skirmish between us over last year's comedy [*Babylonians*]? What does he do but drag me into the Council Chamber and

> batter me with his bilious trumped-up charges, raging, roar-
> ing like a cesspool in spate till it all but drowned me.

And later in the same play we learn that Cleon also charged him, regarding *Babylonians*, with denigrating Athens. He accused him of exposing distinguished foreign visitors to scandalous ridicule to at the City Dionysia. But that charge is not true of *Acharnians*, since it is playing at the Lenaea.

> Gentlemen, I ask you, beggar that I am — not to mention as
> well a writer of comedies — that you be not aggrieved if I
> address Athenians (in a comedy, of all things!) on the subject
> of the State. For not even comedy can divorce itself wholly
> from what is right; and what I say, though it may not be
> palatable, it will be right. This time, at least, I can speak
> freely, without fear of charge by Kleon that I slander the city
> in the presence of foreigners. As it happens, there are no for-
> eigners here; we are alone, among ourselves, this being the
> Lenaian Festival, the time being the dead of winter, and the
> rivers, as it were, being frozen, impeding travel.

MacDowell notes that this charge of embarrassing Athens "is not unlikely [and] that the play did include abusive comments on Kleon," but "the tradition of personal ridicule in comedy made it impossible for him [Kleon] to make any formal complaint about that." In effect, then, the charge was dropped by virtue of being invalid.

So much for *Babylonians*, about which, as a play, we know little, and just a bit more about its historical effect.

COMEDY AS SERIOUS

In the history of the development of Old Comedy, Aristophanes in particular realized that comedy need not be limited to the mindless. Many of his predecessors and colleagues seemed to think so. He believed comedy would benefit from a serious side as well. And so, he looked to tragedy for guidance. There he found a dramatic structure that frequently called for "the restoration of true cosmic order," to use Kenneth McLeish's inspired phrase. "In tragedy," he says, "the hero is often the one who has perverted cosmic order, and its restoration involves him in suffering. In comedy the perversion of natural order has been caused by others; the hero is often the only 'sane' being in an insane world, and his restoration of order leads to rejoicing."

THE HERO OUT OF STEP

The opening prologue of every existing play by Aristophanes registers a complaint. Most often it is by the very person, male or female, who will bring about the restoration of the world that is out of joint. In *Acharnians*, as has already been pointed out, it is the state of disgust and dissatisfaction that Dikaiopolis finds himself in. He has come to the Pnyx at dawn to take part in the Assembly and make certain that the most pressing issue of the day is addressed. He is concerned about the negotiation of peace between Athens and Sparta, to bring to an end the Peloponnesian War that is now in its seventh year. Dikaiopolis laments and is disgusted by the disinterest displayed by the *demos*, the sovereign people of Athens. Instead of appearing at dawn for the meeting of the Assembly, they are at the Agora, the city center and general marketplace, gossiping and wasting time. They will appear at the Pnyx only at the convenient hour of noon, and even then never get around to the discussion of peace. But he has more to complain about. He is a farmer, used to living in the country, which he loves. He relates this as he looks longingly out at the fields of his home from the height of the Pnyx across the walls of Athens. He wants to go back, but he and all country people belonging to Athens have been displaced. They have been brought within city walls for safety's sake to guard against Spartan attack.

This opening scene of discontent is played out in *Lysistrata* as well. It is again just before dawn. And, again, in a monologue, albeit brief,

Lysistrata, alone on stage, castigates the women not just of Athens, but of all Greece (including enemy Spartans). She is upset that they have not responded to her summons to meet on that early morning under the cover of dark. She has had enough of the war, enough of the men of Athens, not to mention all the rest of Greece, being away at war. She has particularly had enough of husbands and lovers being on campaign and not in their wives' or lovers' beds. Her message to the women of Greece? To stage a strike, a sex strike, against their husbands and lovers. She wants them to deny their men their beds and bodies. With no sex on the horizon, Lysistrata is convinced, men will throw down their weapons and return to their women. And the war will end, and the order of the world — at least the Greek world — will be restored. Much the same situation prevails in *Sex and the Assembly* (ca. 392). Praxagora, again before dawn, awaits the arrival of the women who, dressed as men, in their husbands' clothes, will appear at the Assembly. There they will bring about legislation to transfer power to themselves. They will then save Athens from male mismanagement.

And then there is Strepsiades in *Clouds II*. It is before dawn, and Strepsiades, sleeping in the same room with his son finds he cannot sleep. He returns again and again to the thought of his son, who is driving him farther into bankruptcy by his lavish spending. The play, as Henderson puts it, concerns "the growth of untraditional forms of scientific enquiry and of new techniques in the education of young men, particularly rhetorical training, and depicts these as useless, immoral, atheistic, and therefore dangerous to Athens." In the end, Strepsiades burns the Blabatory (a progressive education laboratory run by Socrates). This is his revenge against Socrates for his danger to Athens and the perversion of Athens' young men with the new learning.

DOUBLE TROUBLE

There are also those plays that begin with two disaffected characters who are destined by their author to bring about the restoration of their world. This is true in *Birds*, *Women at the Thesmophoria*, and *Frogs*.

Birds begins on a country road some distance from Athens. Euelpides and Peisetairus are Athenians who have grown disenchanted with the city and its government. They are in search of a more equitable place to live their lives. They are out to find Tereus, once a man, now a bird, to advise them. As a bird he has flown over much of the country and may know of such an idyllic place for them to settle in. One of them has a jackdaw on his wrist to guide them, the other a raven.

EUELPIDÊS: (*To his Jackdaw.*) What's that? What? Straight ahead, you say? Toward that tree over there? That one? Eh?

PEISETAIROS: (*To his Crow.*) Ah, blast! Blast you, you fuckin' bloomin' idiot! I'll have your eyes for breakfast for all they're worth to me! (*To Euelpidês.*) This one keeps bawlin' *back*, *back*!

EUELPIDÊS: Back and forth! Back and forth! It'll be the death of us! What's the sense of it, eh? Endless wanderin', this way and that! I can't, can't anymore, I'm all done in, bushed!

PEISETAIROS: And me? What about me? You think I'm keen on takin' fuckin' orders from a friggin' crow? Bein' led about a hundred miles and more, who knows, eh? And in a circle yet, if I'm any judge! Ah, witless old fool that I am!

EUELPIDÊS: And me? My toenails mere nubs, led astray by a friggin' wooly-brained jackdaw!

PEISETAIROS: Just where are we at now I'd like to know. You, of course, could sniff out Athens blindfold!

EUELPIDÊS: Not likely, old friend.

PEISETAIROS: (*Stumbling as he climbs the rocky slope.*) Bloody hell!

EUELPIDÊS: (*On another path.*) Go that way, if it suits you, I'll go this.

PEISETAIROS: Oh, that black-as-bile-hearted Philokratês from the bird market! He must've seen us comin' a mile off! Two old coots, he thought. I'll put one over on them, I will. Swore to us, he did, these two poor excuses for birds would lead us straight to the Honcho Hoopoe, old Têreus. One obol he fleeced us for that jabber-mouthed jackdaw, and three for that other there, and all they're fuckin' good for is nippin' at our fingers. (*To the Jackdaw.*) So what's it now, eh? What are you gawkin' at? Is it straight on into the bleedin' cliff you're tryin' to lead us, eh? (*To Euelpidês.*) Trust me, there's no way in Hadês we'll be friggin' gettin' through there.

EUELPIDÊS: Not a road in sight. Not a path even.

(*The Crow begins cawing excitedly.*)

PEISETAIROS: Just listen to it there, would you. Something about the road it sounds like. Yep, right, she's changed her mind, croakin' up a different tune.

EUELPIDÊS: What's that? Eh? What's it say about the road?

(*The Crow caws very animatedly and begins pecking.*)

PEISETAIROS: Ow! Ouch! Ow! Nothin', except she plans to bite my fingers off at the knuckles! Ow! Bleedin' bloody hell!

EUELPIDÊS: (*To the audience.*) Wouldn't you just know it? I mean, here we are, the two of us, just dyin' to get out of Athens — we get ourselves all fitted out for the trek, bags and baskets and bedding, and the whole caboodle — and what do we do but lose our way? What we have here, you see, gentlemen, is the plight of that fine tragedian Akestor, except fuckin' bass-ackwards, as it were. As a foreigner and non-citizen, he tried every which way to force his way into the city; while here *we* are, dyed-in-the-wool Athenians, of impeccable pedigree, in good standin', mind you, no one tryin' to shoo us off, and what have we done, the two of us, eh, but flown the bloody coop? Not, of course, because we don't like her, Athens, perish the thought. Not because she ain't great and grand and blest in every way, open to each and all to come and see their wealth get eaten away in fines and taxes. No. It's just that grasshoppers put a limit to how long they chitter and chatter away in the fuckin' fig trees — a month, maybe two at most — but not Athenians, oh no, not them. They chitter and chatter their lawsuits in court from womb to tomb. And so that's why we've fitted ourselves out for this trek with basket and kettle and myrtle wreaths — for sacrificial purposes, don't you know. What we're out to find, let me say, is a place free of trouble, without fines, taxes, lawsuits, all that sort of bother; where we can settle and live out the rest of our lives in peace and serenity. It's for that reason we must find Têreus the Honcho Hoopoe, to learn if he knows of any such happy place; if in all his flights he hasn't come upon such a blessèd city.

DIRTY DUTIES

In several other plays, among them *Peace*, the two characters involved in the opening scene of discontent are not the doers of the deed that will bring about the restoration of world order; but, as McLeish notes, "the impatience or despair expressed is against that doer, because he is acting in a strange and unnatural manner."

In *Peace*, in 421, ten years into the Peloponnesian War, the play's opening action shows two slaves working rapidly molding patties out of a trough of donkey-dung, as one of the slaves informs us. It is their duty to provide a seemingly endless parade of such fodder for the enormous Dung-Beetle inside the stable of Trygaius, the comedy's hero, the one currently acting as though quite unhinged, because he is out of step with his society. We are soon to discover that Trygaius is determined to ride the Dung-Beetle off to heaven to speak directly to Zeus to see what can be done to bring peace back to the world.

FIRST SLAVE: (*Rushing from the stable.*) Hurry, hurry, another cake for the beetle!

SECOND SLAVE: (*Handing him something he has just kneaded.*) All right, all right, then, give it to the bugger!

(*First slave rushes back inside.*)

SECOND SLAVE: May it be the fuckin' tastiest cake it ever eats!

FIRST SLAVE: (*Returning immediately.*) Another, hurry, donkey-dung he says!

SECOND SLAVE: (*Kneading, then handing it.*) Another? Here! Another? Bloody hell, you just gave him one! He can't have scoffed it all down already!

FIRST SLAVE: Can't have, eh? Tell me about it! He grabbed it out of my hand, rolled it into a ball with his feet, and downed it like he was a fuckin' wolf! So don't stop, not for anything, hear? No fuckin' way you can make too many. (*He exits hurriedly into the stable.*)

SECOND SLAVE: (*Kneading feverishly; to the audience.*) All you turd-collectors out there? Yeah, you! You could lend a hand, you know? I could fuckin' suffocate up here!

FIRST SLAVE: (*Returning.*) Another, he wants another! From a pretty rent-boy, he says, with a well-pounded ass! Says he likes his turds well-churned.

SECOND SLAVE: Here! (*To the audience as the First Slave goes inside.*) There's one thing, gentlemen, I'll never be fuckin' guilty of — eatin' on the job.

FIRST SLAVE: (*Returning, repulsed by the stench.*) Ugh! More, more, more, goddamn it! Keep it comin'!

SECOND SLAVE: No, by god, I fuckin' won't keep it comin'! I've had it, I'm done, finished! Basta! Not another friggin' noseful of that shit! Bloody Hell!

FIRST SLAVE: Then I'll see to the bilge myself! (*He picks up the kneading trough and takes it inside.*)

SECOND SLAVE: Take it to bleedin' Hadês for all I care! And yourself with it! (*To the audience.*) And any of you knows where I can buy a nose minus nostrils, let me know. But one thing I know for sure: there's no worse workin' for anyone than kneadin' and servin' food all day to a beetle. I mean, who ever heard of a pig or a dog not scoffing down a pile of shit just as it dropped, like nature intended? Not this fucker, though. Oh, no! This one puts on airs, its nose tilted high, don't you know. And there I am, all day, mashin', squashin', kneadin' his precious shit up into a friggin' hamburger patty! You'd think he was a woman is what! I'll go take a peek in now and see if he's done with his dinner. Just a crack, like this, no more, so he doesn't bleedin' see me. (*At the stable door, peeking in.*) Go on, right, that's the way, gobble away till you fuckin' burst! (*Closing and moving from the door; to the audience.*) You should see the way that bugger eats! Hunched over like a wrestler, jaw movin' side to side, his head and hands swivelin' round like this — (*Imitates the action.*) like men twistin' thick ropes for cargo ships.

FIRST SLAVE: (*Bursting from the stable.*) Ah, the vile, stinkin', greedy, repulsive bastard! What god has cursed us with this calamity? At least not Aphrodite, that much I know, nor the Graces neither.

SECOND SLAVE: Fuckin' who, then?

FIRST SLAVE: Zeus, who else? Zeus Who Shoots Lightning Bolt Turds from on High! Who else could have bloody sent this monstrosity?

SECOND SLAVE: By now, you can bet your sweet ass, there's some young pup of a know-it-all in the audience who thinks he's clever and sayin' to his neighbor: "What's all this? What's all this with the friggin' beetle?"

FIRST SLAVE: And some Ionian sittin' next to him chimes in with: "Well, I think it's Kleon it's about; the same Kleon is down in Hadês now scoffin' his own shit." But I'll be goin' in now. It's almost time for the beetle's drink of piss, and I ain't sure I got anymore to spare. (*He exits into the stable.*)

SECOND SLAVE: (*To the audience.*) And I think maybe it's time I explain the plot to all of you out there: kiddies, youngsters with down on their cheeks, citizen men, men of position, the high and mighty, and, last but not least, you supermen types who rule us. My master is mad, mad call I it, yes, but not like you, no, mad quite differently in fact, mad uniquely. He sits around all day with mouth gapin' — like so — ah? — bitchin' — bitchin' at Zeus — bitchin' all day at fuckin' Zeus. "Zeus," he cries, my master, "Zeus, what's all this? What's on your mind, Zeus, what are you up to? Lay down your broom, hear? Don't sweep away all Greece — our men, our young men!" Shh! Quiet! What's that? I hear a voice.

TRYGAIOS: (*From inside the stable.*) Zeus, Zeus, what are you doing to us? What are you doing to your people? Soon you'll have unmanned every city in Greece!

SECOND SLAVE: (*To the audience.*) Aha! There! You see? That's what I'm talkin' about! That's it! His delusions! The same day after day, ever and always! That's the madness I mean. From the very first he went about mutterin' to himself: "How," he said, "how am I," he said, "to go straight on up to Zeus on high — how?" Then he begins havin' light little ladders made, tryin' to climb his way up to heaven, till once he tumbled, straight on down, down and broke his crown, he did, ah! the fool! After that, even yesterday, mind you, he went out god knows where and picked up an Etna beetle — man-size, no less, ah! and brings it home, and puts it in my charge! Not willingly, I assure you — and *that* you sure as Hadês can believe! And now I'm its bleedin' groom, and he sits in there, my master, rubbing it down like it was some thoroughbred colt, and all. "Ah, my little Pegasos," he cries, "soon on your grand wings we'll be payin' great Zeus a visit!" I think I'll take a peek inside now to see what he's up to, my master. (*Peeping through the door of the stable.*) Help! Help! Neighbors! Come quick! My master! He's flyin'! Flyin' about on the beetle's back! Flyin' like he was on a horse! Ah!

And bring back Peace he does, in the form of a lovely young woman.

REALITY AND NONREALITY

Given the hero's dissatisfaction with the realistic state of the world's order at the beginning of the comedy, and then his further isolation when he attempts to set right the world situation that he sees as wrong, he, or she, is forced, as it were, into a condition of nonreality or fantasy. Lysistrata's situation has already been discussed, except for the likelihood that it is a plan that would have seemed to the Athenian audience of the time the demented raging of a lunatic. She has tried, we must assume, realistic means to win peace, but she has been thwarted, outcast, like all of Aristophanes' heroes. And Dikaiopolis is no different. In his case, in *Acharnians*, the Assembly refuses to take his advice to negotiate for peace with Sparta. Stymied in his realistic attempt, he sets out on his own, determined to find his own peace, which, as it turns out, is a private one. His envoy, Amphitheus, returns from Sparta with three possible treaties, treaties that in reality are wineskins, but, in the nonrealistic fantasy world Dikaiopolis has been forced into in order to restore peace, are wineskins pure and simple. In each skin is a vintage wine. The first he tries is a five-year vintage that, when tested, is described by Dikaiopolis as, "Rat piss! Aargh! Repulsive! It stinks of pitch and battleship bilgewater!" When offered the second skin, a ten-year vintage, he retorts with, "Are you in your right mind, man? Are you pullin' my leg or something? It stinks of fucking embassies and allies bullied into submission!" But when he samples the third wineskin treaty, a thirty-year vintage, he tastes it again and again instead of spitting it out as with the others, exclaiming,

> Holy Day of Dionysos! It's nectar and ambrosia is what it is!
> This one speaks to me loud and clear: "No more troop call-ups, no more battlefield rations, no pissin' and shittin' in a fucking hole," it says! "Go where you like, you're free!"
> That's what it says! Ah! This one I like! This one I'll have!
> This one I pour in libation to peace with Sparta.

And so Dikaiopolis resettles himself and his family back in the country, assured no Spartan invasion will do him and his damage. He sets up a country market of his own in which the money that he so loathes has no place and all things are barter items. In short, he make a life for himself and his family that no one can destroy, while outside, beyond his boundaries, the war persists, fueled by Athens' disregard.

The frustrated hero's deed, then, is accomplished by his being forced into a fantasy world. Only there, in Aristophanes' world, can the right action, the moral and transformative deed, be realized. And yet it is imperative that the audience believe that the deed is inevitable, whether it is Lysistrata's sex strike, Dikaiopolis' personal peace treaty, or Trygaius' flight up to Zeus on a giant Dung-Beetle. As McLeish puts it, "We do not need to feel that *we* could fly to Zeus; but we need to feel not only that Trygaius *can*, but that he *must*."

ALL'S WELL THAT ENDS WELL: OR IS IT?

The final scene of an Aristophanes comedy is one of celebration and rejoicing. There is singing, dancing, feasting; the world is right side up again, reality is restored. What was once, in the upside-down world, seen to have been right is now known to have been wrong. The alienation that opened the play has now given way to the cosmic harmony of humankind and nature, as is seen in the celebration that concludes Aristophanes' *Birds*.

(Enter gorgeously clad as royal couple Peisetairos, thunderbolt in hand, and Princess, equally gorgeously clad, with veiled face.)

(Music. Song. Dance.)

BIRDS: (*Sing.*)
> Make room for the groom!
> Get back! Divide!
> Make way for the bride!
> Make room! Make room!
> Fly with me, fly,
> up into the air!
> Circle them round,
> this radiant pair!

FIRST BIRD: (*Sings.*)
> Sing praise to him now
> and the luck that is ours!
> Sing praise to the bride
> on this feast day of flowers!
> Hail Peisetairos,
> King of the Roost!
> Hail radiant Queen,
> you give us a boost!

BIRDS: (*Sing.*)
> Once when Zeus was king on high
> he and the lovely Hera wed,

joined by the Fates with this lovely song
as they were led off to their heavenly bed:
Hymen O! Hymenaios O!
Hymen O! Hymenaios O!

And Eros of the golden wings
accompanied the heavenly pair,
holding taut the chariot reins,
while all around the air rang fair:
Hymen O! Hymenaios O!
Hymen O! Hymenaios O!

PEISETAIROS: (*Sings.*)
Thanks for your songs!
Thanks for your dances!
Thanks to each bird
that for us prances!

FIRST BIRD: (*Sings.*)
Come with us and praise his power,
he who here before us stands;
he who holds earth-shaking thunders,
lightning, and thunderbolt in his hands!

BIRDS: (*Sing.*)
Sing praise to golden lightning's flare,
Zeus' immortal fiery shaft!
To thunders that make
earth to quake,
and showers fair
to raise up flowers!
With us our King now holds these powers,
lord and master of Zeus' realm,
keen steersman at our nation's helm!
And with him, hand in hand, is seen
our fair, our glorious, our radiant Queen!
Hymen O! Hymenaios O!

PEISETAIROS: (*Sings.*)

> Come, fellow songsters, feathered tribes all,
> follow us, follow, to Zeus' grand hall!

(*To Princess.*)

> Give me your hand, my pretty love!
> Cling to my wing and we'll soar above!
> But first let's dance a little measure
> and show the world our blissful pleasure!
> And then on pinion I'll raise you high,
> and sail you into the glowin' sky!

(*After a short dance surrounded by all, Peisetairos and Princess dance off followed by the chorus of Birds and all who remain.*)

BIRDS: (*Sing.*)

> *Alalalai! Alalalai!*
> *Io! Io! Paion!*
> *Tênella Kallinikos! O!*
> Greatest, oh greatest of gods!

COMEDY: GUARDIAN OF SPIRITUAL HEALTH

Old Comedy had its inception in the "iambic lampoon," as Jaeger calls it, of Archilochus in the seventh century. It began as personal invective, transforming itself in time into a kind of "public criticism in the new liberty of the Ionian city-state." Attic Old Comedy, the iambic's successor, however, developed itself into "the first critical poetry in the true and higher sense." From its beginning as largely harmless personal taunting of private individuals, it developed into its true nature when it made its appearance in the political arena. In Jaeger's words:

> As known to us at the height of its achievement, [Old Comedy] is a true product of democratic free speech. The

Hellenistic historians of literature realized that the rise and fall of political comedy coincided with those of the Athenian democracy. It never flourished again (least of all in antiquity) after the Greeks had been driven — in Plato's phrase — from an excess of freedom to an excess of unfreedom. But it is not enough to consider comedy merely as an exponent of the free democratic spirit. Comedy was produced by democracy as an antidote to its own overdose of liberty, thereby outdoing its own excesses, and extending *parrhesia*, its vaunted freedom of speech, to subjects which are usually tabu even in a free political system.

Comedy, however, did not stand still, satisfied with its accomplishments. Rather it progressed as its host society progressed, and it rendered all kinds of public criticism. Its concern was not, in Jaeger's words, to "pass judgment on 'political affairs' in the narrow modern sense of the phrase. It discussed politics in the full Greek sense — that is, all questions of universal interest to the community." Jaeger continues:

> When it chose, it censured not only individuals, not only separate political acts, but the entire governmental system, the character and the weakness of the whole nation. It controlled the spirit of the people, and kept a constant watch on education, philosophy, poetry, and music. Thereby, these activities were for the first time regarded as expressing the culture of the nation, and as standards of its spiritual health.

SIC TRANSIT GLORIA MUNDI

Though Aristophanes' comedies may have ended in a blaze of rejoicing at the restoration of cosmic harmony, and the people in the tale may have learned the right from the wrong in the progress of their daily lives, one question remains. What did the people in the Theater of Dionysus in Athens learn from the experience, for Aristophanes' comedies are nothing if they are not didactic. Unfortunately, it must be said that from year to year, from Aristophanes' first play, *Banqueters*, in 427, to the production of *Frogs*, in 405, one year before the end of the Peloponnesian War and the fall of Athens to Sparta, Athens seems to have laughed heartily and, one must assume, knowledgably at his plays. And they held their Aristophanes as their master comedian. But apparently nothing about themselves that he revealed to them in his plays seems to have made much difference. Self-involved Athens went its own way. And that way led to a defeat of a major order. Perhaps laughing at themselves in his plays relieved the tension of war and truth just a bit, but it altered no paths. Athens and its people forged their way forward into destruction.

ACHARNIANS

Acharnians, produced in 425, is Aristophanes' earliest existing play. It is one of several of his that treats a subject dear to his heart: peace. The Peloponnesian War that began in 431, and was not to end until 404, was nearing its sixth year. Athenian financial reserves, as Henderson notes, had run dry by 428. As well, Athens had suffered a devastating plague in 430 that had not yet been conquered. This was the same plague that took Pericles. It is a fair guess that Athenians were beginning to think back on Pericles' assurance at the start of the conflict that it would soon be won by Athenian superiority.

At the opening of *Acharnians*, Dikaiopolis sets a scene for the Athenian audience in the Theater of Dionysus that can only have sounded familiar. He laments two things. First, he explains that the countryside around Athens where he once lived had been devastated by Peloponnesian and Boiotian invasions, forcing country people to live within the city walls of Athens. This was a cramped existence at best, in surroundings alien to their natural habitat. The second thing he laments is the failure of the Athenian Assembly even to discuss the possibility of negotiating a peace.

The name of Cleon comes up as the great obstructer to peace. This is the same Cleon whom Aristophanes detested and who actually appeared in his plays in the flesh: Cleon, who, as Henderson indicates, "successfully championed a more aggressive version of the Periclean policy, playing on the Athenians' pride and desire for revenge and questioning the patriotism of anyone inclined toward a negotiated peace." Dikaiopolis, however, is not one to be easily intimidated. So he sets out to do for himself and his family what Cleon and his cronies have refused to do for Athens: negotiate a peace. In Dikaiopolis' case it is a private peace. Needless to say, Aristophanes does not fail to define the quality of his hero in the name he gives him: "What is right for the city [polis]."

His peace negotiated, Dikaiopolis returns with his family to the countryside. He establishes an open market dedicated to trade with all the cities and states with which Athens is at war. And he celebrates the first Rural Dionysia since the war's beginning. Everything that follows in the play flows from this central decision.

Usually Aristophanes sets up in his plays the disparity between the old and the young. He shows youth versus age, old values versus new values, war versus peace. Of these he most often chooses to side with the old because his heart, one might say, is with tradition. It is with the Athens that survived the Persian invasions. And it is with the strength of character and vision that made Athens by the mid-fifth century the glory of the known world. This was the Athens before the fall from grace and the decline into dirty, colonialist politics. This decline was so abrupt at mid-century that the city scarcely had time to bask in its serene, but lively, greatness. In *Acharnians*, however, Aristophanes sides neither with young nor old, but he pits himself against both. He speaks against the old, who are rigid and unable to change their views that their country is right, quite apart from whether it is or is not. And he rails against those who are prey to, and swept away by, the rhetoric of crafty politicians with their dubious appeal to blind patriotism. By the same token he pits himself against the young. He speaks against

Lamachus, the youthful general, who stands in for the lusty and eager youth of Athens and the prospect of winning self-advancement through honor and glory in battle. The degree to which Aristophanes makes of Lamachus a comic braggart warrior and a fool indicates the degree to which he is disillusioned by Athens' youth. As Kenneth Cavander has said: "Aristophanes saw himself as a lonely voice of clarity and sanity; his task was to bring his countrymen to their senses. The conversion of the charcoal burners [the Chorus of Old Acharnians] from hot fiery hostility to gentle peacefulness makes the play a brilliant demonstration of the rôle of the poet and dramatist in Athenian society." The sorry thing, of course, is that it didn't work. And yet, work or not, the fact that *Acharnians* won first prize at the Lenaea is some indication that the Athenians sensed its rightness.

KNIGHTS

Cleon was much vilified in Dikaiopolis' opening speech of *Acharnians*. He is given an even more thorough going over the following year in *Knights* (424) when it took first place at the Lenaea: A fact even more remarkable, as Henderson points out, considering that Cleon had become more powerful than before. He had made a coup at Pylos by stealing a victory from the real generals. He took as hostage a group of 292 Spartan infantrymen who could be used by the Athenians as bargaining chips to put an end to the annual invasions of Attica. Cleon was hailed as a hero for the deed and given all the perks that that title brought with it. According to Henderson, the deed also vindicated "[K]leon's warlike policies, so that the Athenians now rejected out of hand all proposals to negotiate a peace treaty and instead embarked on an ambitious and aggressive series of campaigns."

But *Knights* is not a castigation of Cleon only. It is also aimed at the society, the *demos*, the people, of Athens who sit calmly by and let Cleon and his sycophants feather their nests by means of bribe taking, embezzlement, blackmail, extortion. They also undermined the very foundation of Athenian society and social justice. They corrupted youth and impoverished the have-nots as well as the haves.

In the play, the people of Athens are represented by the character of rickety old Demos (his name means The People). His house represents Athens. And Cleon is represented by Paphlagon, Demos' new slave from Paphlagonia. Paphlagon is a past master at flattery and at pulling the wool over Demos' eyes. Paphlagon is also out to undermine the good standing of two fellow slaves with their master. They, in turn, determine to put an end to his unhappy influence on Demos by showing him up for the vicious scoundrel he is.

As a result, the two slaves manage to gain access to certain oracles regarding Paphlagon. They learn that he can be overcome only by someone more vile than himself. As happens in comedy, such a person just happens to come along. He is a sausage seller heading for the market to sell his wares. He is viler than vile and vulgar as well. He is happy and proud to have been born in the gutter. The two slaves engage him to carry out their enterprise to denigrate Paphlagon in his master's estimation. Into the process they introduce the aid of the Cavalry of Knights. These are youthful, aristocratic, and noble-minded Cleon-haters. They variously help the Sausage Seller to out-bribe, out-gorge, and out-flatter old Demos.

As it happens, Sausage Seller wins. And in a stroke of comedic luck at the end, he miraculously turns dotty old Demos into a youthful warrior of the glorious days of Marathon. The People have been transformed from senile old men obliging other people's interests into vigorous and vital defenders of the new Athens. They bring this about by turning around the policies of Cleon. Alas, it didn't happen.

Knights is a more bitter and politically more vicious play than Aristophanes usually wrote. Henderson's description of it best sums up Aristophanes' despair: "The play resounds with the noise, the vulgarity, the violence, and the selfish cynicism that for Aristophanes typified the new style of Athenian leadership. As for the victory at Pylos, [K]leon had simply stolen the credit from the real generals. No doubt there were other Athenians, though apparently not a majority, who shared these opinions." As for that stolen victory at Pylos, it appears in the play as a newly baked cake for Demos prepared at Pylos by one of his two other servants, stolen by Paphlagon, and offered to Demos as a gift from him. "As for example," complains the servant, "a few days ago I whipped up a splendid Spartan cake down in Pylos, and no sooner it was baked, he snatched it up, our ass-kissing Paphlagon, and off he trots to present it to our stupid, gullible master — and after all my trouble!"

CLOUDS II

If *Knights* is a conglomerate or summary accounting of Athens as Aristophanes saw it in 424, in *Clouds II*, about 418, he narrows his focus and lashes out at only one social development in Athens. He attacks the New Education, whose end result is at best pseudo-intellectualism and at worst immorality.

In all the other existing plays by Aristophanes the hero is well intentioned and wins out in his mission to bring order to a disordered universe. *Clouds II* differs by featuring a hero whose mission is morally corrupt.

The peasant-farmer Strepsiades has married above his station. His grown son, Phidippides, is now squandering his father's means by living a lavish lifestyle commensurate with his aristocratic mother. He is indulging his passion for racehorses. Consequently, his father enrolls himself in The Thinkery. This is a think tank run by Socrates that teaches, through rhetorical techniques and sophistry, the dubious means that will win for its adherents fame, power, and wealth. With this at his disposal, he believes he will escape having to pay his son's extravagant debts. As it happens, it backfires on him. Rustic old Strepsiades hasn't the capacity to learn what must be mastered. So he enrolls his son to do so for him. Phidippides, of course, being young, learns, so well in fact that when he emerges from his course he doesn't set out to help his father win his cases. Rather, he turns his new knowledge against his father. He proves, with the new unjust and immoral logic he has learned, that a son has every right to beat his father, and he proceeds to do so. In a rage, Strepsiades sets fire to The Thinkery. He burns it to the ground and chases Socrates and his students offstage. The play ends without the conventional song, dance, and merrymaking that traditionally brings to an end Athenian Old Comedy.

As for the Chorus of Clouds, those amorphous denizens of the skies, Cedric Whitman defines them as "a complex symbol representing the atheism, materialism, specious rhetoric, and airy nonsense that the poet [Aristophanes] attributes to Sophistic teaching . . ."

But what about the sophistic Socrates of history, as opposed to Aristophanes' Socrates as enemy to the state? Are they one, or are they quite different creations? As it happens, the historical Socrates was frequently lambasted by writers of Old Comedy, much in the way Aristophanes handles him. He was presented as one of the major corrupters of Athenian youth, as an atheist, immoral, and subversive. But then, comedy by its very nature requires exaggeration. And Aristophanes and his contemporaries never shied away from it. It is said that Socrates himself, seated among the spectators in the Theater of Dionysus in Athens, laughed heartily at his own stage depiction.

It must be said, however, that too much such laying on of exaggeration over too long a time may well come to be taken as fact. The most reliable suggestion that such may have been the case is from Plato, who, in his dialogue *Apology*, in which he describes the death of Socrates by governmental edict, speaks to precisely that point. And as Whitman indicates, "Though one of the most famous of all satires on pseudo intellectualism, the *Clouds II* presents serious problems. The wholesale misrepresentation of Socrates as a professor of the new education has been found hard to explain."

As for the reversal of the Aristophanic peasant hero from a man well and honorably motivated to one eager to learn techniques that are morally dubious, in order to bring about an end to his despair, it may conceivably be a sign that Aristophanes felt that even his heroes were selling out along with most of the rest of Athens.

WASPS

The clash between generations is also at the heart of *Wasps*. It was first performed in 422, when Aristophanes was in his twenties and the Peloponnesian War with Sparta was dragging into its ninth year. It is also concerned, like *Clouds II*, with an educational theme. The old way of life is represented by Procleon (Cleon-lover), the new by Anticleon (Cleon-hater), father and son respectively, old and young. Procleon, much like Demos in *Knights*, represents the people of Athens. He is passionate in his devotion to jury duty, and, furthermore, he has never acquitted anyone. His son Anticleon does everything possible to keep the old man at home and out of the courts, but without success — until he is "in a long debate," as Whitman describes it, "he convinces him that a juryman is not an all-powerful magistrate and that he and his fellow jurors (costumed as wasps [representing certain attributes of Athenian jurors]) are the dupes of Kleon's regime." Convinced though he may be by his son's argument, Procleon is still unable to renounce his addiction to litigation and proceeds to set up a home court in his courtyard, where he tries a family watchdog for pilfering a Sicilian cheese. He is tricked, however, by his son into an acquittal of the dog and feels that his career as a juryman has come to ruin.

His former life now a thing of the past, Procleon reluctantly allows his son to introduce him into his own lifestyle, the luxurious life of high society with its drinking parties, rich clothes, and effeminate, unmanly ways. However, despite having been groomed in the proper etiquette by his son, Procleon makes a shambles of the occasion. He gets drunk, liberally insults all present, and takes off for home with the flute girl, accosting everyone along the route. There can be no doubt that the next day Procleon will find himself in court, this time on the opposite side of the proceedings, and learn what it is like. But

Anticleon will most likely learn something as well: that the life he has led and wanted to introduce his father into is as problematic and morally indefensible as his father's former life. David Barrett states the situation:

> In the second half of the *Wasps* we see clearly that, for all their simplicity and gullibility, it is Prokleon and his fellow jurymen who stand for the old-fashioned virtues, for the values that made Athens great in the days of the Persian Wars. Their pride, their obstinacy, their severity, their austerity, and above all their courage and virility — can Athenians afford to let these qualities go out of fashion? "I don't *want* to be given a good time," says Prokleon early on in the play. He is proud of his chilblains, proud of his tattered old cloak that lets the north wind through. . . . In everything except his gullibility Prokleon is a better man than his son, as the latter learns at last when he finds himself flat on the floor. When Prokleon does get drunk, he does it in truly heroic style. And tomorrow, after he has faced his ex-colleagues in court and Antikleon has forked out the money for the fine, not one but two men will be the wiser for their experiences.

PEACE

Peace was written in 421. It was first produced by Aristophanes in the same year at the Great, or City Dionysia in Athens, and with it he took first prize. As its title indicates, Aristophanes had again taken up the subject that informed several of his plays, the first being his earliest existing play, *Acharnians*.

The possibility of peace now, however, was not so lightly dismissed as it was in 425 when *Acharnians* was produced. In the year of *Peace*, Athens had suffered major defeats at Delium and Amphipolis, and, as Thucydides narrates in his *History*:

[T]hey no longer possessed the same confidence in their strength which had induced them to reject previous offers of peace, in the belief that their good fortune at that time would carry them through to final victory. They were also apprehensive about the allies, fearing that they might be encouraged to revolt on a more serious scale, and they regretted that they had not seized upon the excellent opportunity of making peace after Pylos.

It was only two weeks after the production of *Peace* that the Peace of Nicias was ratified between the Athenians and the Peloponnesians. It had been on the table since the previous summer. This ended the first phase of the Peloponnesian War. The Peace was meant to last for fifty years. In reality it lasted for six.

Peace is the tale of Trygaius, a simple peasant farmer (whose name means vintner). It is concerned with the state of Greece and with the war that seems never to end. He has acquired a gigantic Dung-Beetle (his Pegasus for his heroic deed). He intends to fly up to heaven riding the Dung-Beetle to enquire of Zeus why he is determined to wipe out humankind. When he arrives, however, he learns that Zeus and the other gods have deserted and taken off for elsewhere, far distant from man and his problems. Furthermore, Zeus has given over heaven to War and his crony Hurly-Burly. But no sooner has War gone off to find another giant pestle with which to grind down the Greeks than Trygaius instructs a Chorus of Greek Farmers to excavate the goddess Peace from her confinement in a deep cave. This they do. They also free her two companions, Harvest and Holiday, both of whom War had driven from their home among humankind. In returning them to Earth, Trygaius brings plentitude and joy. One, Holiday, he gives to the members of the council; the other, Harvest (his occupation being grapes), he marries at the play's conclusion in a festive and holiday mood.

Though the play ends happily in dancing and song, Henderson is correct in stressing that what the play says is that "peace is attainable, but only if all Greeks make a final, concerted effort to secure it." That indeed the negotiations could fail is indicated by the obstacles thrown in Trygaius' path as he struggles to achieve his mission, as well as by the fact that there are still obstructionists, at home and abroad, who resist.

BIRDS

Birds took first prize at the Dionysia in 414 and is noted for several things. In the first place, it is, as Henderson points out, the longest of the comedies to come down to us from antiquity. It also displays a greater concern for structure and unity of plot than the existing plays of Aristophanes that precede it. As in his other plays about unlikely "heroes," things are set moving by the voicing of a complaint. There is the creation of a fantastic idea to surmount it, and the idea's implementation. Various episodes show the results of the implementation and the hero's idealistic victory in returning the cosmos to order. Notable, too, is the play's lack of political attack. This is probably explained by the relative calm of the time of the Peace of Nicias, a fifty-year truce that lasted for only six, 421–415. Moreover, Cleon, Aristophanes' favorite subject of political attack, was dead. And there was no political figure in Athens important or dangerous enough for Aristophanes to bother about. That situation, Aristophanes must have reasoned, could be handled by the minor comic playwrights around, and didn't require the master. During this period, evidence indicates that Aristophanes turned his art to mythology and subjects of an apolitical nature. "To be sure," writes Henderson, "there is plenty of topical satire [in *Birds*], but all of it is incidental to a fantasy that soars above the world's particulars to a conjured realm, where the most familiar hierarchies of empirical reality — earth and sky, nature and culture, polis and wilds, humans, animals, and gods — are blurred, reordered, or even abolished, and whose hero attains power surpassing even that of the gods."

Birds opens with two average, elderly male Athenian citizens on the road. They are in flight from Athens in search of a city that is better and more accommodating to live in. They are Peisetairus and Euelpides, whose names, respectively, mean "Persuasive" and "Hopeful." They are out to find Tereus, once a man and king of Athens. He has now been transformed into a Hoopoe, and he is king of the birds. In his flights throughout the land, they feel certain, he must have come upon someplace that is better than Athens. And they want his help in finding it, their ideal, dreamed-of state. But Tereus proves of little help. Every place he mentions presents a drawback, some connection that relates it to Athens and her influence.

Peisetairus then has an idea, a true inspiration. He proposes that the birds establish their own utopia, a city in the sky, Cloudcuckooland. From there they will rule the world, cutting off from the gods the smoke of the sacrificial offerings of men. This will starve the gods into submission. The birds are skeptical and resistant. Peisetairus, true to his name, persuades them that, in fact, they are the gods. It was they who preceded the Olympian gods as the first to be created, and the Olympians stole their sovereignty from them. Convinced, the birds set about building their city in the air. They persuade mankind of the birds' rightful divinity, and they force the famished gods into capitulation. In the end, Peisetairus, now having grown wings, finds himself master of the universe, with Zeus' Basileia ("Empire," or "Sovereignty") for his princess bride.

All the other of Aristophanes' plays before and after *Birds* are set in Athens and have as their mission to satirize Athens and its people with unabashed intimacy. They provide a firsthand knowledge of the cunning, duplicity, and political malfeasance that now constitutes Athens' daily existence. *Birds*, however, takes place outside of Athens. Its satire, therefore, is not so intimate. Aristophanes' central focus is on the "Athenian" ingenuity of Peisetairus. He focuses Peisetairus' sharpness in dealing with the situation of Athens and the war, a move not unlike Dikaiopolis' in negotiating a personal peace between himself and Sparta. *Birds* is, in effect, an answer to the Athenian Empire that is rapidly, in 414, coming undone. The Peace of Nicias had been violated and ended the previous year and the war was on again. The first round of the disastrous Sicilian Expedition in 415 to capture Sicily and its fortunes in order to bolster Athens in its desperate decline had led to a monumental failure. The second and final defeat was shortly to come, in 413. Peisetairus, disgusted with Athens and the state of things, leaves the city and manages to create an empire of his own. It is a universal one, no less, all of creation, one to put that of Athens to shame. It is an empire powerful enough even to depose the gods. It is a creation, on Aristophanes' part, that satirizes the very idea of Athenian arrogance. It is a reflection of where Athens, in its imperial fantasy, had indeed arrived. As if to ram this insight home, Aristophanes, as Whitman points out, informs us that Basileia, Peisetairus' bride, "has all the attributes of Athena, including thunderbolts, and of Athens, such as navy yards and finance commissioners." It's quite as if Aristophanes and Thucydides were on the same track of thought. In his *History of the Peloponnesian War,* Thucydides notes that Pericles was said to have remarked that having once had an empire, one is conditioned to retain it, even if unwillingly.

LYSISTRATA

With *Lysistrata*, in 411, at the Lenaea Festival, Aristophanes turns again in his existing plays to the political realm for inspiration. He is again, as in *Acharnians* and *Peace*, in search of a negotiated settlement of hostilities. He is looking for not only local unity but Panhellenic unity as well. The massive Athenian armada was totally defeated in 413 at Sicily. This resulted in the loss of almost incalculable numbers of men, material, and wealth. The prospect for Athens looked more grim than ever. But "grim" may not do justice to the sense of despair that settled over the city. "Black" is perhaps a more apt description of the worst state of affairs that Athens had found itself in since the Persian Wars. A. H. Sommerstein describes the situation:

Late in 413 B.C. the news reached Athens of the total destruction of their expeditionary force in Sicily. They had no navy and, it seemed, no hope. Sparta had already occupied the strong point of Decelea in Attica, and the Athenians daily expected her naval forces, or those of Syracuse, to appear before the Piraeus; and Athens' subject allies . . . seized the opportunity of changing sides.

For all of the humor that buoys up this most popular of the comedies of Aristophanes, *Lysistrata* is interlarded with a despondency that reveals Athens at its most desperate. Even the hilarity of a sex-strike staged by the women not only of Athens, but all of Greece — even enemy Sparta — against their men until they make peace, is a sign of that desperation. It is a reduction to the absurd. This is even more so for the fact that it is led by a woman. The possibility of such an event could not be entertained, even remotely, by the phallocentric Athenian male. So improbable is the situation that Aristophanes has dreamed up, that to consider *Lysistrata* a dream is itself not so far-fetched a possibility.

On the one hand, the dream can function either in a compensatory or a cautionary capacity. As compensation, the dream makes light of a serious state of affairs on the conscious level. This helped lessen the tension generated by that real-life crisis. In its cautionary or warning capacity, the dream reveals through the unconscious the seriousness of the real-life situation. Athenians had chosen to ignore it because it is too frightening, or debilitating, to deal with. It is tempting to suggest that *Lysistrata* serves both functions simultaneously. It allows an Athenian in the Theater of Dionysus to laugh at the situation in which he is trapped, namely a war that refuses to end, rather than succumb to hopelessness. At the same time, it warns him of the degree of danger he is in by virtue of the real-life impossibility of what the dream proposes: a sex-strike called by the women to bring the peace. So urgent is the dream's message that there is at least one irreconcilable loophole in its construction. The sex-strike could not have happened because the men of Greece are all at war. They are not at home, and therefore cannot be subject to the strike. In a word, the logistics are just not right.

It is, of course, not the audience in the Theater of Dionysus in 411 having this dream, it is Aristophanes. Here the intuitive artist is the dreamer for his society, and he delivers that dream through his art. Unfortunately for Athens and her people he was only good for a laugh to distract them from more serious matters.

WOMEN AT THE THESMOPHORIA

Women at the Thesmophoria was first performed in the same year as *Lysistrata*, 411. It was shown at the Greater Dionysia rather than at the Lenaea. It was a play not about politics and war. It must have been deemed better fare for the foreign contingent that always attended. The state of things in Athens had not changed appreciably since *Lysistrata*, except for a coup d'état by the Four Hundred, an anti-democratic group, which lasted only a few months.

The Thesmophoria was an all-female religious festival that was held annually throughout most of Greece — in Athens during the fall. It lasted for three days. The goddesses central to the event were Demeter and her daughter, Persephone, goddesses of fertility. The first and second days were most likely devoted to the descent of Persephone into the Underworld in the fall and winter of the year. This was followed, on the third day, by her rise, bringing with spring new birth and fertility to the Earth. The day in between was devoted to a strict fast from food and wine.

Contrary to the women in *Lysistrata* and *Sex and the Assembly*, the women of the play are doing nothing wrong, or even exceptional. They aren't taking into their own hands matters that are exclusively the business of men. They are doing what the ordinary women of Athens do, celebrating a religious festival, from which, it must be emphasized, the male is strictly excluded.

The sole subject of the play is Euripides, the great tragedian of fifth-century Athens, and his alleged misogyny. The women of Athens meet on the occasion of the Thesmophoria. They are planning to try Euripides (one must assume in absentia) and to condemn him to death for his (in their eyes) defamation of women, and for slandering the entire female sex in his plays. Euripides learns of the impending event. He attempts to persuade the effeminate tragic poet Agathon to disguise himself as a woman and infiltrate the trial to plead in Euripides' defense. He fails but manages to persuade his kinsman, Mnesilochus, to take on the task. He gets a dress and various female accessories borrowed from Agathon's wardrobe. At the trial, Mnesilochus' defense of Euripides consists of enumerating all of the vile and despicable ploys, deceptions, ruses, and misdeeds that Euripides failed to mention. His identity is exposed. He is apprehended and tied naked to a post under the surveillance of a Scythian guard. The remainder of the play consists of attempts by Euripides to free him by using various escape scenes from his own plays. Euripides plays the role of the liberator, and Mnesilochus picks up the cues of the one being liberated. He finally succeeds by distracting the guard with the charms of a naked dancing girl. In the end, Euripides and the women agree to a compromise.

Contrary to what one might think, Euripides was probably not offended by Aristophanes' audacity in his satire. He most likely felt complimented by the considerable research into his body of work that the play called for.

FROGS

Frogs was written and first performed in 405, one year before Athens' collapse and the end of the war that had raged, with minor interruptions, from 431. Along with the imminent fall of the state — for no Athenian could logically have expected otherwise — there was also the decline and eventual fall of Old Comedy. This form of comedy was devoted to the criticism of the state and of its corruptors, a comedy that could only subsist in a democracy. *Frogs*, then, was the last of Aristophanes' genuine Old Comedies.

The art of Attic Tragedy was already dead, or nearly so. Euripides had died the year before, and Sophocles died only a few months before the performance of *Frogs*. Only Sophocles' son, Iophon, was left, we are informed in the play. In response to this calamity, Aristophanes, in *Frogs*, dispatches Dionysus, the god of the festival and of theater, to take upon himself the "heroic" task of descending to the Underworld to bring back to earth Euripides, his favorite tragic playwright. This would revive tragedy lest it die out entirely. The great tragic poets of Athens were not merely poets. They were Athens' teachers as well, their moralists, and guides in adversity as well as prosperity. They may have had no Bible, but they had Homer to teach them honor, honesty, and that greatest of all Greek virtues, *arete*. *Arete* signified always striving for the highest and the best. This was the only nobility.

Now that Athens was on its last legs it had need of its teachers as never before, even more than at Marathon and Salamis. And so Dionysus sets out, for the good of Athens, to seek out Euripides to advise Athens in her extremity. Accompanied by his sidekick Xenthias, together they experience some of the most ribald situations in Aristophanic comedy. They meet the bawdy Heracles, who will advise them on the dangers of the trip. They meet the hostess of an inn at which the wily Heracles misbehaved (as one would expect him to) on his trip to Hades. Dionysus' disguise as Heracles doesn't help him with said hostess. They meet Charon, too, steersman of the skiff that ferries the dead across the river Styx to Hades, but he will ferry only Dionysus. Xenthias, being only a servant, will have to walk. Finally in the Underworld, Dionysus becomes the judge of a contest between Euripides and Aeschylus regarding who will occupy the Underworld Chair of Poetry, which is currently being occupied by Aeschylus.

In the course of this contest, Dionysus realizes that what Athens in peril most needs is not the clever, revisionist, and utilitarian

Euripides to advise it, Despite his wisdom. Rather, Athens needs the nobility and greatness of heart of the moralist that Aeschylus was in life and still is in death. He may have been dead for a quarter of a century, but his vision of man's potential greatness is what Athens most lacks. And so it is Aeschylus who accompanies Dionysus back to Earth and life to teach Athens and her people what they most need to learn to survive.

For all the comedy of *Frogs*, however, its core resides in the great central speech, the *parabasis*, delivered by the Leader of the Populace of the Underworld. He speaks to the assembled audience in the Theater of Dionysus, in effect, to Athens herself, regarding what it must do to survive.

It is only right, I say, rightly the duty of our sacred chorus to offer advice to the city, enlightened instruction for its own good. First, we believe that it is incumbent upon us that every Athenian citizen should be made equal, and that their every fear be removed. As for those caught in the net of deception by Phrynichos, those who were tripped up by him and his wiles and led astray, let us, as a body, permit them to join us once again and slough off the errors of their past. All of which is to say, let us forgive them. They made mistakes, yes, but that was long ago. Let us offer them now the honor of amnesty. There should be no one in the city deprived of his civic rights. It is reprehensible to think that veterans of but a single battle at sea — former slaves — no matter how bravely they fought — should be awarded a rank higher than free-born citizens — as happened when they were given such rights at Plataea, transformed — as a result of one engagement — from slaves into masters. Which is not to say, of course, that I criticize that action, I do not, they deserved it, and it was the only sensible thing you did. Still — and I say it again — there are those others, men who have fought at sea, and often, too, fought beside you, and not them only but their fathers, and their fathers' fathers before them, blood relatives to you, men who made one mistake and were summarily disenfranchised! What of them? Are they to remain so forever? Or ought they, too, to be pardoned their one mistake when they beg you for it? Listen to me, then, Athens, for you are the wisest of cities, master your rage, and in so doing embrace as kinsman and citizen every man who fights at sea beside us! At this moment, Athenians, when our city founders in a sea of troubles, if we choose to parade our uncompromising arrogant pride, we will, one day, be judged to have acted not wisely. [. . .] It has come increasingly to mind in recent days that the city treats the best of its citizens much like it treats the old coinage, the noble silver drachma, but the new gold as well. Both, to say the least, are splendid examples — unalloyed, honorable, honest stuff, the finest of all coins everywhere — true-minted and tested. Clink them and they ring with clear bell tones. The fly in the ointment, though, is that we make no use of them — not use them. We use instead these coppers — wretched, debased coinage, struck yesterday or the day before, or the day before that ill minted, a genuine eyesore, a disgrace to us and our country. And it is no different with our citizens, the same citizens we readily acknowledge our finest; men born of splendid ancient stock, honest, honorable, just, proud; men well educated in the wrestling schools, in choruses, and the arts. And what do we do? Do we use them, this enviable resource in our midst? No. We do not. We scorn, we reject, we outrage them, choosing to use in their rightful place men as base as our copper coins — bad men, badly minted, badly born, aliens, the latest arrivals, men we wouldn't earlier have selected to serve as public scapegoats in our rites. The time is late, oh blind and misguided nation, but better late than never. Change your ways, choose good men to lead you, good men for public service — be led, I say, by Reason. That way, if you win, you will have universal respect; and, if you fail, you will have failed in the eyes of all with honor!

The tragedians of Athens were moral leaders of the people — teachers, preachers, wise men. They held in their hands, for two hours each, each day of the festival, the hearts, souls, and minds of the people of Athens, molding them in the image of honor and nobility. It was what they did. It was what the people expected of them. But they were now gone, and of the greats, albeit a comic playwright, only Aristophanes remained. He must have looked around (as he did regularly in most of his plays) and said to himself that what is happening isn't right, and that if I don't speak out now, before it's too late, I will have only myself to blame. And so he spoke out, loudly and eloquently, to Athens, and Athens didn't listen. It continued giving ear to the fools who were dragging it down — politicians, orators, sophists who continued weaving their clever, plausible, but in the end fallacious arguments. Not too many months after the first production of *Frogs*, Athens fell.

SEX AND THE ASSEMBLY

Between *Frogs*, in 405, and *Sex and the Assembly*, most likely in 392, a gap of some dozen years, Aristophanes wrote four additional plays, plays in which, possibly, he further left behind the form of Old Comedy that he had raised to its zenith. In this he paved the way for the new form of comic writing to be known as Middle Comedy.

With the fall of Athens in 404, the stage of Old Comedy was vitally affected. As W. G. Arnott notes, "the loss of imperial power and political energy was reflected in comedy by a choice of material less intrinsically Athenian and more cosmopolitan." In *Sex and the Assembly* and *Wealth* the comic chorus has begun to atrophy and the *parabasis* has disappeared entirely. In place of specific lyrics written for the chorus, pre-existing songs would be interpolated. A manuscript, for example, might simply, as in *Sex and the Assembly*, indicate "song." Gone, too, Arnott informs us, are the dangling leather phalluses and the grotesque padding that were so much, and so bawdy, an element of Old Comedy. In form, then, these final existing plays by Aristophanes may be considered the earliest examples of Middle Comedy.

The war over, things improved to some degree, but it was a long road to recovery. Barrett lays out the most devastating events of the post-war period.

> Under the pro-Spartan oligarchs who then came to power in Athens, a reign of terror ensued: in the course of the year 404 no fewer than 1,500 Athenian citizens were executed, and 5,000 were banished. A force of exiled democrats was raised by Thrasybulus, and after some months of civil war they re-entered the city and the democratic constitution was restored (September, 403). Since then there had been a slow recovery, but since 395, through her defensive alliance with Boeotia and other Greek states, Athens had again been involved in inconclusive hostilities with the Spartans. The state of war dragged on, a drain on money and manpower: the future was obscure, the economy shaky, counsels divided, and the glory of Athens (it seemed) a thing of the past.

What precisely it was — historically speaking — that prompted the writing of *Sex and the Assembly* is uncertain because of its slightly uncertain date. In any event it cannot have been a favorable time for Athens, for the question the play addresses is how to save the city — the same question, Barrett points out, that was asked at the end of *Frogs* in 405, and for good reason. In any case, whatever the situation, it was sufficiently urgent to prompt *Sex and the Assembly*.

Like Lysistrata (whose name means "disperser of armies"), Praxagora (whose name means "she who is active in the marketplace," which is to say "in public life") takes male matters into her own hands. But there is one difference: Peace comes about. Praxagora's action is meant to be permanent. Lysistrata's action was meant to last only for a time, till the desired end of the war. Praxagora's action was to take over the governance of the city and to be permanently in charge. It is as if Aristophanes is saying: "The peace has come, so let us have peace. But men are returning to their old ways, we are in conflict again with our former enemies, so now let's let women have a chance." And let them have their chance, he does.

Under Praxagora's guidance, the women of Athens meet before dawn, dressed in the clothes of their sleeping husbands, with beards the better to hide their identity. They march to pack the Assembly, and they succeed in getting passed the proposal that the government be handed over to the women. This passes unilaterally because it is the only thing that has never been tried.

The government established by the women is a communal one. Private dwellings are abolished. Wealth, private property, and goods are appropriated and are to be distributed according to need. Children are to be raised communally. In addition, a community of males is established with the stipulation that a man may enjoy a young woman, but only after he has first satisfied any old woman who may want him. This way not only the young and beautiful will be served, but all ages and descriptions. It is this law that leads to the play's longest, funniest, and rowdiest scene. A young man comes to serenade and make love to a young woman he is infatuated with. But he is intercepted by several old hags who demand their own legal rights. In the process they all but tear him to pieces, in the end dragging him off, communally, to pay them their due.

As a play, *Sex and the Assembly* is not one of Aristophanes' best constructed. It lacks a truly functional comic chorus and has no *parabasis*. Characters are introduced, never to return; subjects are raised, never to be revisited. The end result is something like chaos — but what wonderful chaos! The play may well be the funniest of Aristophanes' existing plays. It has the distinction of being the bawdiest and most uninhibitedly sexual of them all, including *Lysistrata*. It is also, by far, the most scatological. So uninhibited is it and so outrageous that it rises above its spirited — indeed inspired — low comedy. It leaves audiences gasping for air, as has been proven in a number of recent productions.

WEALTH

Wealth tells the story of an Athenian farmer, Chremylus, a man of the landed class, but just barely. His interest in the world of economics is understandable. Chremylus, accompanied by his servant Carion, has just been to consult the oracle of Apollo at Delphi. His cynicism with regard to life and society has brought him to question the value of honesty in human dealing. He has an only son. He questions whether it is not better to raise him to be a criminal than an honest man, for what does honesty bring one? Apollo's response is typically obscure. He is told to take home with him the first man he comes upon on leaving the sanctuary. As it happens, the individual he meets and tries to make friends with is a blind, decrepit old man. He eventually reveals himself to be the god Wealth, who long ago was blinded by Zeus so as no longer to be able to tell good men from bad, or bad from good.

Chremylus has the ingenious idea that he will restore sight to Wealth, and in doing so reintroduce into the world the just distribution of wealth, rather than the indiscriminate distribution that has prevailed since the long-ago blinding. His sight restored, Wealth will once again associate with good men only, instead of with good and bad alike. The result will be that only the good will be rewarded with wealth. Wealth, however, is terrified of Zeus and Zeus' retribution. But, counters Chremylus, Zeus is powerless. He argues that it is only because of the prospect of wealth that mankind worships him. Without man's worship, Zeus is nothing.

Wealth is convinced, and Chremylus takes him to Asclepius' temple for the cure, but not before the ugly hag Poverty enters to protest mightily. Men, she insists, need poverty in order to make something of themselves by struggling to escape it. Without poverty they are nothing. By having escaped it, they become useful citizens of the state. Chremylus, however, doesn't buy it, and he and Carion take Wealth off to the temple.

Once Wealth's vision is restored, there follow several scenes that indicate the result of the cure. The world's economic system is reversed, and economic justice is again in place. All good men gain wealth, all bad men become penniless. The evil are out of work and suffering. The good are now as prosperous as formerly they were penurious. And Zeus' former messenger, Hermes, out of a job, will apply to be employed as kitchen staff in Chremylus' house. In the end, Wealth is reinstalled into his former place, in the treasury of the Parthenon on the Acropolis where originally he resided. And the play ends with that staple of all comedies, general celebration.

It is clear from the preceding description that the audience to whom Aristophanes was playing in 388 was not the audience he addressed in the fifth century before the end of the Peloponnesian War. Kenneth Cavander describes the change:

> For wild fantasy [*Wealth*] substitutes moralizing allegory, and its plot faithfully works out the intellectual implications of the debate between Wealth and Poverty. Aristophanes was clearly responding to a new audience, with new expectations — a bourgeois public, interested not in political controversy but in private concerns of money, personal behavior, and security. The character of [Karian], foreshadowed by Xanthias in *Frogs*, is the prototype for the "clever slave" of New Comedy, and the usurpation of Zeus by [Wealth] is a perfect image of the change in Athenian life between the fifth and the fourth centuries B.C.

But there were other changes introduced in *Wealth* that were just as pronounced. As Henderson indicates: "Also pointing to later comedy are the play's bland humor, linguistic simplicity, straightforward morality, relative lack of topicality and satirical animus, and the characters' commonplace names and personalities." He adds that it was precisely these characteristics that recommended the play to later antiquity, the Middle Ages, and the Renaissance, making it the most popular of Aristophanes' works.

Another major change in the transition from Old Comedy to Middle Comedy had to do with the gods. Early on, Aristophanes appears to have believed, as Sommerstein says, in the "benevolent protection of the gods." But as time went by, and the war continued, and Athens suffered, the benevolence of the gods came under scrutiny. Evil, he once believed in his young days — war in particular — was the result of a combination of human wickedness and human stupidity. This is exemplified in *Knights* in the characters of Paphlagon and Demos. Put an end to the war, advised Aristophanes, or rid the city of Cleon. Or at least return to the old morality and concept of public service that prevailed at the time of Marathon and Salamis. The gods' protection, however, began soon to be questioned in Aristophanes. By the time of *Birds* (414) the gods, for their lack of benevolent protection, are put in their place for their low estimate of humanity. And yet, perhaps paradoxically, it is still going strong in *Frogs* (405), where Aeschylus is chosen by Dionysus to return to Earth in order to reestablish the moral order of Marathon and Salamis. By the time *Wealth* comes along, however, the gods are little regarded. Zeus, not human wickedness and stupidity, is accused of bringing evil into the world by virtue of his blinding of Wealth. For this he is displaced and roundly denounced as an autocrat for his tyrannical subversion of economic justice.

DRAMATIC MOMENTS

from the Major Plays

These short excerpts are from the playwright's major plays. They give a taste of the work of the playwright. Each has a short introduction in brackets that helps the reader understand the context of the excerpt. The excerpts, which are in chronological order, illustrate the main themes mentioned in the In an Hour essay.

BIRDS (414 BCE)
opening scene

CHARACTERS

Euelpides (Euelpidês)
Peisetairus (Peisetairos)
Xenthias (Xanthias)
Manodorus (Manodoros)
Bird-slave
Tereus (Têreus)

[In this whimsical play, two old men are frustrated with the current state of their home city, Attica. The two men, Peisetairus and Euelpides, decide to leave Attica. Following their birds, a crow and a jackdaw, they want to find a new city free of trouble. Eventually, they come upon Tereus, the king of the birds.]

(A desolate, wooded, rocky landscape some distance from Athens. A steep, rocky cliff at the rear. Enter an exhausted and frustrated Peisetairos and Euelpidês, the first with a Crow on his wrist, the latter with a Jackdaw. They are followed by their slaves, Xanthias and Manodoros, loaded with baggage, bedding, cooking equipment, and other paraphernalia.)

EUELPIDÊS: *(To his Jackdaw.)* What's that? What? Straight ahead, you say? Toward that tree over there? That one? Eh?

PEISETAIROS: *(To his Crow.)* Ah, blast! Blast you, you fuckin' bloomin' idiot! I'll have your eyes for breakfast for all they're worth to me! *(To Euelpidês.)* This one keeps bawlin' *back, back*!

EUELPIDÊS: Back and forth! Back and forth! It'll be the death of us! What's the sense of it, eh? Endless wanderin', this way and that! I can't, can't anymore, I'm all done in, bushed!

PEISETAIROS: And me? What about me? You think I'm keen on takin' fuckin' orders from a friggin' crow? Bein' led about a hundred miles and more, who knows, eh? And in a circle yet, if I'm any judge! Ah, witless old fool that I am!

EUELPIDÊS: And me? My toenails mere nubs, led astray by a friggin' wooly brained jackdaw!

PEISETAIROS: Just where are we at now I'd like to know. You, of course, could sniff out Athens blindfold!

EUELPIDÊS: Not likely, old friend.

PEISETAIROS: (*Stumbling as he climbs the rocky slope.*) Bloody hell!

EUELPIDÊS: (*On another path.*) Go that way, if it suits you, I'll go this.

PEISETAIROS: Oh, that black-as-bile-hearted Philokratês from the bird market! He must've seen us comin' a mile off! Two old coots, he thought. I'll put one over on them, I will. Swore to us, he did, these two poor excuses for birds would lead us straight to the Hon-cho Hoopoe, old Têreus. One obol he fleeced us for that jabber-mouthed jackdaw, and three for that other there, and all they're fuckin' good for is nippin' at our fingers. (*To the Jackdaw.*) So what's it now, eh? What are you gawkin' at? Is it straight on into the bleedin' cliff you're tryin' to lead us, eh? (*To Euelpidês.*) Trust me, there's no way in Hadês we'll be friggin' gettin' through there.

EUELPIDÊS: Not a road in sight. Not a path even.

(*The Crow begins cawing excitedly.*)

PEISETAIROS: Just listen to it there, would you. Something about the road it sounds like. Yep, right, she's changed her mind, croakin' up a different tune.

EUELPIDÊS: What's that? Eh? What's it say about the road?

(*The Crow caws very animatedly and begins pecking.*)

PEISETAIROS: Ow! Ouch! Ow! Nothin', except she plans to bite my fingers off at the knuckles! Ow! Bleedin' bloody hell!

EUELPIDÊS: (*To the audience.*) Wouldn't you just know it? I mean, here we are, the two of us, just dyin' to get out of Athens — we get our-selves all fitted out for the trek, bags and baskets and bedding, and the whole caboodle — and what do we do but lose our way? What we have here, you see, gentlemen, is the plight of that fine tragedian Akestor, except fuckin' bass-ackwards, as it were. As a foreigner and non-citizen, he tried every which way to force his way into the city; while here *we* are, dyed-in-the-wool Athenians, of impeccable pedigree, in good standin', mind you, no one tryin' to shoo us off, and what have we done, the two of us, eh, but flown the bloody coop? Not, of course, because we don't like her, Athens, perish the thought. Not because she ain't great and grand and blest in every way, open to each and all to come and see their wealth get eaten away in fines and taxes. No. It's just that grasshoppers put a limit to how long they chitter and chatter away in the fuckin' fig trees — a month, maybe two at most — but not Athenians, oh no, not them. They chitter and chatter their lawsuits in court from womb to tomb. And so that's why we've fitted ourselves out for this trek with basket and kettle and myrtle wreaths — for sacrificial purposes, don't you know. What we're out to find, let me say, is a place free of trouble, without fines, taxes, lawsuits, all that sort of bother; where we can settle and live out the rest of our lives in peace and serenity. It's for that reason we must find Têreus the Honcho Hoopoe, to learn if he knows of any such happy place; if in all his flights he hasn't come upon such a blessèd city.

PEISETAIROS: Psst! Hey!

EUELPIDÊS: What?

PEISETAIROS: This crow keeps cawin' upward. Up there.

EUELPIDÊS: So's the jackdaw. Keeps lookin' up like it was tryin' to point something out to us. I suspect the place is swarmin' with birds. Make a ruckus and we'll fuckin' find out soon enough.

(They approach the smooth cliff-face and Euelpidês kicks it with his foot.)

PEISETAIROS: Right, kickin' the rock makes the birds to flock.

EUELPIDÊS: Bangin' it with your head'll make twice the noise.

PEISETAIROS: Use a stone then, dummy.

EUELPIDÊS: Whatever. (*He knocks with a stone on the cliff-face.*) You, in there! Boy! Boy!

PEISETAIROS: "You, in there!"? "Boy!"? "Boy!"? What are you doin'? You don't call the Hoopoe "boy!"! You say: "Oh, Hoopoe!" Say it!

EUELPIDÊS: (*Knocking again.*) Oh, Hoopoe! (*To Peisetairos.*) I suppose you'll be makin' me knock again! (*He knocks.*) Oh, Hoopoe!

BIRD-SLAVE: (*Within.*) Who's there? Who's croaking for the master?

(*The cliff-face door is opened and the Bird-Slave appears with a beak distressingly large. In terror Xanthias and Manodoros drop the baggage and flee to the side, Peisetairos collapses, and the Crow and Jackdaw fly off in a flurry of squawks.*)

EUELPIDÊS: (*Terrified.*) Fuckin' bloody hell! Check out the beak on that bird!

BIRD-SLAVE: (*Equally terrified.*) Oh lordy, a pair of bird-nappers! Aiiiiii!

EUELPIDÊS: (*To Peisetairos.*) I don't like the looks of this — nor of *him*!

BIRD-SLAVE: You men are as good as dead!

EUELPIDÊS: Sorry, we're not mortals.

BIRD-SLAVE: You could have fooled me. What, then?

EUELPIDÊS: I'm a Yellow-Belly Screecher from distant Libya.

BIRD-SLAVE: Bull!

EUELPIDÊS: Bull to you, crap to me. Look at my droppings.

BIRD-SLAVE: And him? What kind's he?

PEISETAIROS: Me? I'm a Brown-Bottomed Shitterling from, from — from far off Phasis.

EUELPIDÊS: (*To the Bird-Slave.*) But what in the name of Elysium might *you* be?

BIRD-SLAVE: (*Announcing proudly.*) A Bird-Slave is what I am.

EUELPIDÊS: Bird-Slave, hm? Some fighting-cock get the better of you, did he?

BIRD-SLAVE: No-no, no such thing. When my master changed from man to Hoopoe, he longed dearly that I be a bird as well, to tend him, a — mmn — major-domo, so to say.

EUELPIDÊS: Since when do birds need butlers?

BIRD-SLAVE: Yes, well, this one does, definitely. Having once been human, you know, he got so used to it, as humans will. He'll have a longing, say, for sardines, and so off I'll wing it to Phalêron to fetch them fresh. Or he'll crave a spot of lentil soup, and off I'll flap for a ladle and tureen.

PEISETAIROS: (*To Euelpidês.*) This customer's a regular skyrunner. Say, skyrunner, how about poppin' inside and rousin' your master for us?

BIRD-SLAVE: Out of the question. Not once he's started his after lunch nappy time.

PEISETAIROS: Eats a lot, does he? Then sleeps it off?

BIRD-SLAVE: Oh, mercy, no such thing. A modest repast of myrtle-berry and gnat does him nicely.

PEISETAIROS: Wake him.

BIRD-SLAVE: He won't be amused. I'll wake him. (*He goes back into the cliff-face.*)

PEISETAIROS: (*Calling after, though not too loud.*) And damn you to Hades for scarin' the shit out of me!

EUELPIDÊS: And my jackdaw, too! Scared shitless!

PEISETAIROS: I think it was *you*, Mr. Yellow-Belly Screecher, was scared shitless and let your jackdaw go!

EUELPIDÊS: Oh? So it wasn't *you* fell down on your fuckin' face and let your bleedin' *crow* go?

PEISETAIROS: My crow go! No!

EUELPIDÊS: Where is it then?

PEISETAIROS: Flew off, is what!

EUELPIDÊS: All on her own, eh? Ah, ain't you the brave one!

TÊREUS: (*From within; booming.*) Open the glade, do you hear! I'm coming out!

(*Enter Têreus through the cliff-face door. He has the magnificent triple crest of a Hoopoe, a Hoopoe's wings, a face with a sharply hooked beak, and a sparse coat of feathers. The rest of his body is human.*)

EUELPIDÊS: (*In a fit of laughter.*) Holy fuckin' Heraklês, what *is* this? Look! The plumage! And that tiara crest!

TÊREUS: Who is it seeks me?

PEISETAIROS: (*Also laughing.*) Looks to me the gods did a real number on you, man!

TÊREUS: I trust you're not laughing at my plumage. I was, you know, a man once, my friends.

EUELPIDÊS: (*Trying to stifle his laughter.*) Oh, no, it ain't *you* exactly we're laughin' at.

TÊREUS: Then what's so funny?

EUELPIDÊS: Well, to tell the truth, it's that — that beak.

TÊREUS: Blame Sophokles for that. It's how he treats me, Têreus, in his tragedies.

EUELPIDÊS: Ah! I see! I see, then, yes! Then you're Têreus. Be you bird or — peacock? I mean, considerin' the get-up.

TÊREUS: Oh, bird, yes; bird, of course.

EUELPIDÊS: Excuse me for askin', but what's happened to your feathers?

TÊREUS: Oh, well, they fall out, you see.

EUELPIDÊS: Disease, distemper? You've been ill?

TÊREUS: Oh, certainly not. We birds lose our feathers in the winter and grow new ones. Molting it's called. But tell me, gentlemen, who are you?

PEISETAIROS: Us? Who are we? We're humans.

TÊREUS: Humans. I see. What sort? I mean, where is it you hail from?

PEISETAIROS: From the city that makes fine warships.

TÊREUS: Aha, Athens. In that case, I do hope you're not jurymen.

PEISETAIROS: You've got *that* right! *Not* jurymen. It's the other way around. Fact is, we're jurorphobiacs.

TÊREUS: I didn't know they grew that sort in Athens.

EUELPIDÊS: Look hard enough, you still find a few in the country.

TÊREUS: Now then, what brings you here?

PEISETAIROS: We've come for advice.

TÊREUS: May I ask what about?

PEISETAIROS: Well, we figured that you was human once like us, and like us had debts, and, what's more, like us, you liked getting out of paying 'em — the debts, don't you know. Then all of a sudden you ditch all that for the life and times of a bird. Well, now, it seems like, to us, you have the unique perspective of both man *and* bird, having flown far and wide over land and sea. And that's why we've come to you for advice. We was wonderin', do you know of a city where things are a bit more — what should I say? — more comfortable? Cushier, perhaps, more like a soft and fleecy blanket to curl up in real comfy and take a snooze?

TÊREUS: A city greater than Athens do you mean?

PEISETAIROS: Greater? Not hardly. Just one where life's a bit — easier.

TÊREUS: Ah well, then, it's an aristocracy you seek.

EUELPIDÊS: Me? Not likely. Just the thought makes my tummy turn somersaults.

TÊREUS: Then what sort of city do you fancy?

EUELPIDÊS: Oh, one in which a really bad day would go something like this. A friendly neighbor comes knockin' at my door one morning and says: "Once you and your kids have had your baths, hurry on over to my house, I'm celebratin' a wedding. Come nice and early, and don't forget; for if you do, I won't be seekin' your help when I'm on the skids."

TÊREUS: I can see what a glutton you are for hard times. And you?

PEISETAIROS: Oh, I'll take a serving of the same.

TÊREUS: Example?

PEISETAIROS: Well, I'd like a city where the father of some beauty of a boy comes up to me livid with rage and shouts in my face: "A fine thing, this, I must say!" he yells at me. "You meet my boy comin' out of the gymnasium all fresh and glowin' from his bath, and what do you do but nothing! Nothing! You don't talk to him, you don't kiss him, you don't cuddle him or even tickle his friggin' balls! And you consider yourself a family friend?"

TÊREUS: Mercy me, the troubles you do long for! And yet there is such a place would suit you both. On the sea, in fact. The Red Sea.

EUELPIDÊS: No-no, oh no! Spare us the sea! No summons and sub-poena servers for us! Arrivin' by boat at dawn poundin' our door doin' his bleedin' duty. I think it's an inland Greek city we're lookin' for.

TÊREUS: Well, there's always Lepreon in Elis.

EUELPIDÊS: Lepreon? Oh I think not. Never been there, but I've seen their leprous poet Melanthios, and that's enough for me.

TÊREUS: How about Opous, then, with the Opuntians?

EUELPIDÊS: If Opuntios comes from Opous, count me out. I wouldn't live there for a sack of gold. Ah, but you know what I'm wonderin'? What's it like, life here with the birds? You should be an expert on that.

TÊREUS: Life with the birds? Not bad, really; not bad at all. In the first place, we don't have money, banished it quite out of existence.

EUELPIDÊS: Ah! Life's worst complication, dispatched in a flash!

TÊREUS: And in gardens we feed on white sesame, myrtle berries, poppy, and watermint.

EUELPIDÊS: Sounds to me like a never-endin' feast!

PEISETAIROS: (*Suddenly; inspired.*) Listen! Oh, I've got it! I do think I've got it! Listen to this! Just listen! I've just had a dream, a vision of what life could be like for you birds, the power that can be yours, if only you follow my advice!

TÊREUS: And what is it you advise us?

PEISETAIROS: What is it I advise you? Well, for starters, stop flyin' about all over the friggin' place with your bleedin' beaks hangin' open. It looks ridiculous and does nothin' to gain you respect. For example, back home in Athens if we see some ditherin' dimwit and ask: "Who's that?" Someone will answer with: "That? Why, that's the local birdbrain! Fluttery, flighty, facetious, ants up his friggin' pants and not least up his ass, and never known to settle in the same place twice."

TÊREUS: Yes, well, I guess that would do the trick. What would you
    suggest?

PEISETAIROS: Found your own city.

TÊREUS: City? Birds? Birds found a city? But what kind of city would
    that be?

PEISETAIROS: What a stupid, what a really stupid bloody question!
    Look down there.

TÊREUS: Yes, I'm looking.

PEISETAIROS: Now up, look up.

TÊREUS: I'm looking.

PEISETAIROS: Now swivel your head around.

TÊREUS: Yes, well, that's really smart. All I need is a sprained neck at
    my age.

PEISETAIROS: What did you see?

TÊREUS: See? Well, I saw clouds and — and a great mass of sky.

PEISETAIROS: Aha, and there you have it!

TÊREUS: Have it? Have what?

PEISETAIROS: The province of the birds, is what! Their *sphere*!

TÊREUS: Sphere? I don't un —

PEISETAIROS: All right, their *space*, then, call it what you will —
    sphere, space — all that counts is that things pass through it. So,
    then, what do you do? You settle this sphere-space, you surround
    it with walls, you fortify it, and there it is, *voilà*! your city, and what
    a vast city it will be! And what's more, you'll have the upper hand
    on humans, just as now you have the upper hand on grasshoppers.
    Or, to be blunt, you'll rule the human race. As for the gods, well,
    you'll cut them off, cut 'em off clean, like we cut off the Melians
    when we took them by siege. The gods? They'd starve to death.
    Simple as that.

TÊREUS: How's that?

PEISETAIROS: Why, you'll do in the sky the same as men do on earth.
    You'll remember, I'm sure — you were a man once — how when
    you wanted to visit the oracle at Delphi, you needed a visa to cross

through Boiotian land? Well, so now it will be the same with the gods. Either the gods pay you annual tribute, or you will refuse the aroma of roasting thigh bones to rise up through your apace when men offer sacrifice.

TÊREUS: Ohohohoho! Grand! Glorious! Oh by the Earth, by Nets, by Gins and Springes, never have I heard a cleverer idea! And given that the birds agree, I'll join you in founding this city!

PEISETAIROS: Now, who's going to pitch the idea to 'em?

TÊREUS: Why, you! You, of course! I admit, when I took over here, they chirped and twittered all sorts of nonsense. Ah, but in the meantime I've taught them Greek, and so they're no longer barbarians.

PEISETAIROS: I see, yes, well — and how will you call 'em into General Assembly?

TÊREUS: Couldn't be easier. I'll dash off here into my thicket, rouse my nightingale wife, and together we'll send out a call. Once they hear, they'll be round, as you say, in a fucking jiffy. (*He enters the thicket and clambers up the brush-covered cliff-face.*)

PEISETAIROS: Dearest of birds, do hurry, I beg you! Into the thicket and rouse your Lady Nightingale!

****

from **LYSISTRATA** (411 BCE)
opening scene

CHARACTERS

Lysistrata
Calonike (Kalonikê)
Myrrhine (Myrrhinê)

[In this scene, Lysistrata is devising a plan to end the Pelopoennesian War. It involves gathering the women of Greece together and telling them to refuse sex with their husbands. Only when the men have signed a peace treaty will the wives greet their husbands again in bed. Below, Lysistrata discusses this plan with her neighbor Calonike.]

(Early morning. The entrance to the Akropolis, Athens. LYSISTRATA enters, looks around and sees no one.)

LYSISTRATA: Wouldn't you just know it? Invite them to a Bakkhic revel, a rowdy romp for Pan, or a fertility bash at Genetyllis' shrine at Kolias and they'd flock here like pigeons! Streets crammed, crowds pushing and yelling, tambourine and drum ringing! And so, I look around me and see not a single woman in sight. It figures.

(Enter Kalonikê.)

Well, except perhaps for one of my neighbors here. 'Morning, Kalonikê!

KALONIKÊ: Same to you, Lysistrata. Why, whatever's wrong, my dear? This isn't like you, child. I mean, knitted brows and all? Screwing up your face? It doesn't suit you.

LYSISTRATA: Women! I'm so ashamed of them, Kalonikê! Ashamed of *us*! Listen to men and we're the source of all mischief. Sometimes — like now — I wonder if maybe they're right, after all. Oh, I'm so furious I could burst!

KALONIKÊ: You may just have a point there.

LYSISTRATA: Here I invite them to a meeting of the first importance, and where are they, those women, the fools, but still at home in bed?

KALONIKÊ: Don't fret it, honey, they'll be here. Give 'em time. It's no easy task for a woman to fly the coop. There's the hubby to see to. You bend over backwards to tend *his* needs — and sometimes in the other direction, if you catch my drift. And then there's waking the slaves, or putting the baby to bed, or bathing, washing, feeding it.

LYSISTRATA: I know, I know, yes, but there are other things should matter more!

KALONIKÊ: But, dear, why exactly are you calling this meeting? I mean, what's up? Is it something big?

LYSISTRATA: Let's say, it's nothing piddling.

KALONIKÊ: And juicy?

LYSISTRATA: Fairly bursting with juice, so to speak.

KALONIKÊ: Big *and* juicy, then?

LYSISTRATA: Big *and* juicy.

KALONIKÊ: Oh, the fools! The idiots! Then why aren't they here? What are they waiting for?

LYSISTRATA: Shame on you, Kalonikê! I meant no such thing! Well, not exactly that, I suppose. If I had, we'd have a mass of screaming female monkeys on our hands. No, it's — it's an idea I've thought hard about, tossing and turning in bed at night, trying to sleep.

KALONIKÊ: It must be worn to a frazzle by now, all that tossing and —

LYSISTRATA: (*Passionately.*) Oh, Kalonikê, the salvation of Greece — all of Greece — lies in *our hands*, the hands of *women*!

KALONIKÊ: Oh, save us, has it actually come down to that?

LYSISTRATA: Yes, it depends on *us*, our country's future. It's up to us whether the Peloponnesians are annihilated —

KALONIKÊ: I'm for that, all right, no more Peloponnesians! Good!

LYSISTRATA: — and the Boiotians eliminated —

KALONIKÊ: Yes, well, but let's not be overhasty. Let's not do in the eels that come from their waters. Yummy!

LYSISTRATA: — and then there's us Athenians — but I won't say it, you know what I mean. But if we come together here, we women, Boiotian, Peloponnesian, we Athenians — well, together we can save Greece!

KALONIKÊ: But we're women, Lysistrata, what can *we* do? Let alone something clever, something intelligent. We sit around the house all day looking pretty for our husbands, saffron dresses, make-up, see-through shifts and fancy slippers.

LYSISTRATA: And there you have it, Kalonikê! That's it! That's *exactly* what will rescue Greece! Saffron dresses, fancy slippers, perfume, rouge, and our own special see-through little nothings!

KALONIKÊ: Well, I don't quite —

LYSISTRATA: I'll see to it that no men living today will ever again raise their spears against each other —

KALONIKÊ: In which case I'll be dyeing some dresses saffron!

LYSISTRATA: — nor hoist their shields —

KALONIKÊ: And dress in a little nothing!

LYSISTRATA: — nor raise their swords!

KALONIKÊ: I'll need some fancy slippers!

LYSISTRATA: So then, why aren't the women here now?

KALONIKÊ: Now? They should have sprouted wings and flown here ages ago!

LYSISTRATA: Oh, my dear, you'll see soon enough, they'll prove themselves Athenian to the core. Everything they do, they do too late. Why, there's not a woman here yet from the shore, or even Salamis.

KALONIKÊ: Oh, you know those shore-women types. They're in the saddle at dawn and flying high.

LYSISTRATA: Those women I counted on being here first, the Acharnians? They aren't here either.

KALONIKÊ: Theogenes' wife I saw consulting her shrine to Hekate, so she's bound to come.

(Enter groups of Women from various directions, among them Myrrhinê.)

Over there! Look! Some coming now!

****

from **LYSISTRATA** (411 BCE)
an excerpt

CHARACTERS

> Lysistrata
> Calonike (Kalonikê)
> Myrrhine (Myrrhinê)
> Five Wives
> Cinesias (Kinêsias)
> Manus
> Baby
> Very Old Men
> Very Old Women
> Spartan Herald

[In this scene, Lysistrata is with several of the women who have sworn off their husbands sexually. Myrrhine is one of the women. After a few words are exchanged between the women, Myrrhine's husband, Cinesias, enters the scene. He is aflame with passion for his wife, desiring her very badly. But Myrrhine refuses his advances, after initially teasing him.]

> *(Enter Lysistrata high on the battlements, scanning the horizon, when suddenly she spots something in the distance and cries out in her delight.)*

> *(During the following scene the Very Old Men and the Very Old Women withdraw to opposite edges of the stage space, the Very Old Women gathering up their own discarded clothes as well as those of the Very Old Men.)*

LYSISTRATA: Everyone! Hurry! See what's coming!

> *(Enter excitedly the Five Wives, along with Kalonikê and Myrrhinê.)*

KALONIKÊ: Lysistrata, what is it?
FIRST WIFE: Why were you shouting?

SECOND WIFE: What?

LYSISTRATA: A man! Coming this way! Do you see? There! Hm, and from the look of it, he's primed and ready for battle!

KALONIKÊ: (*To herself.*) Aphroditê, mistress, goddess of Kypris, Kythêra, and Paphos, be with us now, don't abandon us, keep us on the straight and narrow, onward and ever upward!

THIRD WIFE: Where is he, this man, whoever he is?

LYSISTRATA: (*Pointing offstage.*) There! Do you see? By Dêmêter's shrine!

KALONIKÊ: So he is! I see him now! But, lordy, Lysistrata, who is he?

LYSISTRATA: Take a good hard look, girls. Anyone recognize him?

MYRRHINÊ: Oh, no! Oh, god! Yes! It's my husband! It's Kinêsias! Oh!

LYSISTRATA: (*To Myrrhinê.*) Well, dear, you know what to do. Tease him, taunt him, terrorize, torture him, but one thing you *won't* do — give him what he's so fucking horny for.

MYRRHINÊ: I'm true to my word, girl! Count on me!

LYSISTRATA: And I'll stick around to help with the taunting and torture. Quick now, ladies, out of sight!

(*Exeunt Wives, Kalonikê, and Myrrhinê.*)

(*Enter Kinêsias in a state of pronounced discomfort, his gigantic stage phallus swaying in rigid erection. He is followed by Manês, a slave, carrying a Baby.*)

KINÊSIAS: Ow! Oh! Ah! Ouch! Better the fucking rack than this friggin' horn of plenty!

LYSISTRATA: Halt! Who goes there?

KINÊSIAS: (*Pissed.*) Me is who goes here, that's who!

LYSISTRATA: A man?

KINÊSIAS: (*Brandishing his phallus angrily.*) Bloody hell, woman, what are you, blind?

LYSISTRATA: Off with you then! Out of here!

KINÊSIAS: *You?* Telling *me* to clear out? Who the hell are you?

LYSISTRATA: Captain of the guard.

KINÊSIAS: In that case, captain, I beg you on my knees, bring out
    Myrrhinê to me.

LYSISTRATA: (*Mocking.*) "Bring out Myrrhinê to me," he says! And just
    who might you be, may I ask?

KINÊSIAS: Kinêsias. Her husband.

LYSISTRATA: Kinêsias! Well, why didn't you say so? Kinêsias, darling,
    your name's a household word around here! It's always on your
    sweet wife's lips! She can't suck at an egg or tongue the dangling
    sack of a fig without remarking: "Ah, how this reminds me of my
    Kinêsias!"

KINÊSIAS: (*To himself; in agony.*) Fucking shit!

LYSISTRATA: It's true, by pudgy little Eros, it is, I swear. And whenever
    the subject of men pops up, she always chimes in with: "No man
    can hold a candle to my Kinêsias!"

KINÊSIAS: (*All but writhing.*) Bring her, oh, bring her to me, bring her!
    Please!

LYSISTRATA: You, uh — got anything for me?

KINÊSIAS: (*Taking his phallus in hand.*) If this is what you want, lady, it's
    yours on loan. Otherwise, here. (*He tosses up to her a purse of coins.*)
    It's all I've got.

LYSISTRATA: Very well, I'll call her for you. (*Exit.*)

KINÊSIAS: Hurry it up! Please! Please hurry! (*To the audience.*) Take it
    from me, life's been no bundle of joy lately. The pits. The absolute
    pits. Ever since she up and deserted me. I go home, I'm in pain,
    empty rooms, empty bed, empty table. Everything empty. Nobody.
    Not even the food tastes good. I'm horny as Hades and in perma-
    nent need of a lay!

MYRRHINÊ: (*From offstage, meant to be heard.*) I love him, I love that
    man, I do! But he just doesn't want it, doesn't want my love! Please,
    Lysistrata, no, I don't want to go down to him!

(*Enter Myrrhinê on the battlements.*)

KINÊSIAS: Baby? Sweetheart? Myrrhinê? What are you doing to me?
    Why? Come down here now, you hear? This minute!

MYRRHINÊ: Down there? No. Definitely not.

KINÊSIAS: Hey, you, Myrrhinê, I'm tellin' you! Get on down here! *Fast!*

MYRRHINÊ: Why? You don't need me. Not really.

KINÊSIAS: Fucking bloody hell, woman, not need you? I'm a friggin' basket case!

MYRRHINÊ: Sorry. I have to go.

KINÊSIAS: No! Wait! Stop! At least listen to the baby! Goddamn kid, come on, yell, will ya? (*Pinching the Baby roughly.*)

BABY: (*Bawling.*) Mama! Mama! Mama!

KINÊSIAS: What is it with you, woman? It's your baby! Suddenly you don't love him? Uh? Your own baby? Your heart suddenly froze? Six days he hasn't had a wash or a feed!

MYRRHINÊ: *Me?* Cold-hearted? What? It's *him* I pity, with a father who doesn't look after him!

KINÊSIAS: You come down here, woman! Now! You're nuts! Fuckin' nuts! So get down here and see to this kid of yours!

MYRRHINÊ: What's a mother to do! (*Disappears from the battlement.*)

KINÊSIAS: (*To the audience.*) Actually, I think she looks younger, by a long way, you know? And — and her eyes. They're sexier, too — sexier than I remember at least. And as for the crap she's just laid on me — well, it only helps to stoke my fire.

(*Enter Myrrhinê through the gates and goes immediately to the Baby, taking it in her arms.*)

MYRRHINÊ: (*Baby talk.*) Poor little thing with such a mean old daddy; now give us a kiss, mommy's little snookums!

KINÊSIAS: (*Approaching her.*) Why do you act like this anyway? Stupid. Really stupid. Listening to those hens. Holing yourself up with a bunch of loonies. Hurting not only me but yourself. (*He tries to caress her breasts.*)

MYRRHINÊ: Hands off the merchandise if you know what's good for you.

KINÊSIAS: And you should see the house. Going to wrack and ruin. Everything — your stuff, mine — it's a pigsty.

MYRRHINÊ: I couldn't care less.

KINÊSIAS: Your wool being pecked to bits by the hens, and you don't *care*?

MYRRHINÊ: You got that right.

KINÊSIAS: And the rites of Aphroditê? Her holy rites? How long's it been since we did it? Uh? Oh, Myrrhinê baby, won't you come home? Please?

(Kinêsias embraces Myrrhinê, who slips from his arms and returns the Baby to Manês.)

MYRRHINÊ: Aha, come home, is it? It's that simple? No. Not till you men make a peace settlement and bring this war to an end.

KINÊSIAS: All right! If that's what they decide, it's what we'll do.

MYRRHINÊ: All right! If that's what they decide, then I'll come home. In the meantime, I've taken an oath to stay here.

KINÊSIAS: But at least let me love you a little. It's been so long.

MYRRHINÊ: Sorry, no go. But at least that doesn't mean I don't love you.

KINÊSIAS: You love me? You do? So then why can't we do it?

MYRRHINÊ: Here, in front of the baby? Don't be silly.

KINÊSIAS: Oh! Well, no, not really. I mean — Manês, get the kid out of here!

(Exit Manês with the Baby.)

There! See? Simple! Vamoose! Can't we get down to it now?

MYRRHINÊ: You out of your mind? Where? There's no place.

KINÊSIAS: Pan's Grotto will do just fine. It's right over there.

MYRRHINÊ: But I'd have to purify myself before going back up. How would I do that? The Akropolis is sacred ground.

KINÊSIAS: There's a spring nearby. You could do it there.

MYRRHINÊ: You're asking me what? To break my oath?

KINÊSIAS: Fuck the goddamn oath, I'll take the blame!

MYRRHINÊ: In that case I'll get us a bed.

KINÊSIAS: So what's wrong with the good old ground?

MYRRHINÊ: I may love you, Kinêsias — just not on the ground. (*Exit into Pan's Grotto.*)

KINÊSIAS: (*To the audience.*) Well, at least she loves me. That's something.

MYRRHINÊ: (*Returning with a camp cot.*) Here we are, then. So lie down, why don't you, and I'll be getting off my —

(*He lies down.*)

MYRRHINÊ: Or no, I think — I think we need a mattress. I'll get one.

KINÊSIAS: Stuff the bloody mattress! Who needs it?

MYRRHINÊ: But surely we can't — not on the bare cords, I mean. How absolutely grizzly.

KINÊSIAS: All right, then, but at least a kiss.

MYRRHINÊ: (*Gives him a peck.*) There.

KINÊSIAS: (*As she exits into the grotto.*) Holy Heraklês! Bring the mattress! Hurry! (*Kinêsias writhes in pain on the cot as Myrrhinê returns with the mattress.*)

MYRRHINÊ: Here we are! Up with you now! There. Lie back down and I'll get out of my — oh, but there's no pillow!

KINÊSIAS: Shove the pillow!

MYRRHINÊ: (*As she exits into the grotto.*) Be back in a jiff!

KINÊSIAS: (*To his erection.*) Hold on, old fella, it can't be much longer!

MYRRHINÊ: (*Returning with a pillow.*) Let's raise ourselves up again, sweetheart. (*He groans; she places the pillow; he lies back down.*) There, now, that should be everything.

KINÊSIAS: Oh, I do hope so! Now come to me, my little puss!

MYRRHINÊ: I'm loosening my breast band, darling. Just remember — no reneging on the peace settlement.

KINÊSIAS: I'd sooner die first! I swear!

MYRRHINÊ: (*As if surprised.*) Oh, but where's the blanket?

KINÊSIAS: It's a fuck I fucking need, not a blanket!

MYRRHINÊ: (*Going off into the grotto.*) And you'll have one made right to order, sweets! Back in a jiffy, blanket and all!

KINÊSIAS: Damn the woman and her frigging bedclothes!

MYRRHINÊ: (*Returning with the blanket.*) Up again! Let's get ourselves up!

KINÊSIAS: (*Tense.*) It's been up for six friggin' days! (*He rises as she spreads the blanket, then lies back down.*)

MYRRHINÊ: Shall I rub you down with scented oil, honeybun?

KINÊSIAS: I think I'll pass on that.

MYRRHINÊ: I'll do it anyway. (*She goes into the grotto.*)

KINÊSIAS: (*Between his teeth.*) Oh god, please, let her spill it, and let's get on with it!

MYRRHINÊ: (*Returning with a round jar of oil.*) Your hand, dear, hold it out now — (*Applying a few drops.*) — now rub it in. I'll do the shoulders. (*She begins anointing his shoulders and massaging.*)

KINÊSIAS: (*Smelling his hand.*) This is terrible! I hate it! What a piss ant awful smell!

MYRRHINÊ: (*Pretending to sniff his shoulder seductively.*) Oh, clumsy little me! I've brought that rancid Rhodian variety!

KINÊSIAS: Never mind, it's all right, darling, really.

MYRRHINÊ: You just go on babbling while I — (*She runs off into the grotto.*)

KINÊSIAS: Blast the creature who first invented scent!

MYRRHINÊ: (*Returning with a long, slender, cylindrical bottle.*) Here's a lovely tube of a sweeter aroma.

KINÊSIAS: I have my own *not*-so-sweet-smelling tube, thank you! Now get your fucking ass into this bed, woman, and —

MYRRHINÊ: (*Interrupting.*) Coming, darling, coming, just slipping off these slippers. And you will remember to vote for peace, won't you?

KINÊSIAS: Oh, there'll be peace, all right, you can —

(*She slips back into the Akropolis and the gates clang shut behind her as Kinêsias turns to reach out for her.*)

Fuuuuuuck! Shit! Cocksucker! Done in! Done down! Done dirty! By a woman yet! Pumped up, primed, and abandoned! Holy shit!

(During the following, the Very Old Men, still naked, and the Very Old Women, now dressed and carrying the clothes of the Very Old Men, take up a more prominent position, and the cot of the previous scene is removed.)

(Music. Song. Dance.)

KINÊSIAS: *(To his phallus; sings.)*

> My laddie's alone
> demanding attention,
> peeled to the bone,
> requiring subvention.
> What will you do now,
> laddie, my love?
> Who will you screw now,
> heavens above!
> Who will raise you,
> who will praise you,
> who will graze you,
> haze you, daze you?
> My willy's sore,
> my nuts in rut,
> I need a good whore
> to rattle my butt,
> or a good bum-boy
> to settle my gut!

VERY OLD MEN: *(Sing.)*

> By Sodom and Begorra, lad,
> you've been diddled mighty bad,
> we feel for you, alas!
> Cock a-twirling, balls a-swirling,
> head and gut together whirling,
> we feel for your cute ass!
> Where's now the bitch to scratch your itch?

KINÊSIAS: (*Sings.*)

>> Run away, the ruddy witch!

VERY OLD MEN: (*Sing.*)

>> You've no one now, you've lost your luck.

KINÊSIAS: (*Sings.*)

>> I'll have no early morning fuck!

VERY OLD MEN: (*Sing.*)

>> These crafty women stoke our fire,
>> then leave us in situations dire!
>> The witches, the bitches,
>> they hitch us, they ditch us!
>> They leave us in cramps,
>> the devious tramps!

KINÊSIAS: (*Sings.*)

>> No, she's sweet, my love, my dear!

VERY OLD MEN: (*Sing.*)

>> Sweet? No, vile! Get your ass in gear!

KINÊSIAS: (*Sings.*)

>> Vile? Yes! Almighty Zeus,
>> lift her on high, her taunting caboose,
>> whirl her and twirl her in the turbulent air,
>> like a handful of sand, and hold her there!
>> Then send her down,
>> down to the ground,
>> swirling and whirling,
>> round and round,
>> to land on the randy knob of my cob!

(*Enter a Spartan Herald sporting an erect stage phallus, which he unsuccessfully tries to hide beneath his cloak.*)

(*Music out.*)

****

Aristophanes

THE READING ROOM

YOUNG ACTORS AND THEIR TEACHERS

Aristophanes. [*Complete Plays.*] 4 volumes. Loeb Classical Library. Translated and edited by Jeffrey Henderson. Cambridge: Harvard University Press, 1998–2002.

Bermel, Albert. *Farce: A History from Aristophanes to Woody Allen.* Simon and Schuster, 1982.

Bieber, Margarete. *The History of the Greek and Roman Theater.* 2nd ed. Princeton, N.J.: Princeton University Press, 1961.

Bloom, Harold, ed. *Aristophanes.* Broomall, Penn.: Chelsea House, 2002.

Handley, E. "Comedy." *The Cambridge History of Classical Literature.* Vol. I. Cambridge: Cambridge University Press, 1985.

Harman, Edward. The Birds *of Aristophanes Considered in Relation to Athenian Politics.* London: E. Arnold, 1920.

Harriott, Rosemary. *Aristophanes: Poet and Dramatist.* Baltimore, Md.: Johns Hopkins University Press, 1986.

Harvey, David, and John Wilkins, eds. *The Rivals of Aristophanes: Studies in Athenian Old Comedy.* London: Duckworth and the Classical Press of Wales, 2000.

Heath, Malcolm. *Political Comedy in Aristophanes.* Göttingen: Vandenhoeck & Ruprecht, 1987.

Littlefield, David J., ed. *Twentieth Century Interpretations of* The Frogs: *A Collection of Critical Essays.* Englewood Cliffs, N.J.: Prentice-Hall, 1968.

Lord, Louis E. *Aristophanes: His Plays and His Influence.* New York: Cooper Union, 1963.

Marianetti, Marie C. *Religion and Politics in Aristophanes'* Clouds. New York: Olms-Weidmann, 1992.

Reckford, Kenneth. *Aristophanes' Old-and-New Comedy: Six Essays in Perspective.* Chapel Hill: University of North Carolina Press, 1987.

This extensive bibliography lists books about the playwright according to whom the books might be of interest. If you would like to research further something that interests you in the text, lists of references, sources cited, and editions used in this book are found in this section.

Redfield, James. "Drama and Community: Aristophanes and Some of His Rivals." *Nothing to Do with Dionysos?* John J. Winkler and Froma I. Zeitlin, eds. Princeton, N.J.: Princeton University Press, 1989.

Renehan, Robert. *Studies in Greek Texts: Critical Observations to Homer, Plato, Euripides, Aristophanes and Other Authors.* Göttingen, Germany: Vandenhoeck & Ruprecht, 1976.

Silk, Michael. *Aristophanes and the Definition of Comedy.* Oxford: Oxford University Press, 2002.

SCHOLARS, STUDENTS, PROFESSORS

Anderson, Carl A. *Athena's Epithets: Their Structural Significance in Plays of Aristophanes.* Stuttgart, Germany: Teubner, 1995

Boughner, Daniel C. *The Braggart in Renaissance Comedy: A Study in Comparative Drama from Aristophanes to Shakespeare.* Westport, Conn: Greenwood Press, 1970.

Bowie, A. *Aristophanes: Myth, Ritual and Comedy.* Cambridge: Cambridge University Press, 1993.

Branham, R. Bracht, ed. *Bakhtin and the Classics.* Evanston, Ill.: Northwestern University Press, 2002.

Colvin, Stephen. *Dialect in Aristophanes and the Politics of Language in Ancient Greek Literature.* Oxford: Oxford University Press, 1999.

Croiset, Maurice. *Aristophanes and the Political Parties at Athens.* New York: Arno Press, 1973.

Dane, Joseph. *Parody: Critical Concepts Versus Literary Practices: Aristophanes to Sterne.* Norman: University of Oklahoma Press, 1988.

David, Ephraim. *Aristophanes and Athenian Society of the Early Fourth Century B.C.* Leiden, The Netherlands: Brill, 1984.

Davidson, Mary. "Transcending Logic: Stoppard, Wittgenstein, and Aristophanes." *Alogical Modern Drama.* Kenneth S. White, ed. Amsterdam: Rodopi, 1982.

De Luca, Kenneth M. *Aristophanes' Male and Female Revolutions: A Reading of Aristophanes'* Knights *and* Assemblywomen. Lanham, Md.: Lexington Books, 2005.

Dick, Aliki. *Paedeia Through Laughter: Jonson's Aristophanic Appeal to Human Intelligence.* The Hague: Mouton, 1974.

Dobrov, Gregory, ed. *Beyond Aristophanes: Transition and Diversity in Greek Comedy.* Atlanta, Ga.: Scholars Press, 1995.

Edmonds, Radcliffe. *Myths of the Underworld Journey: Plato, Aristophanes, and the "Orphic" Gold Tablets*. New York: Cambridge University Press, 2004.

Edmunds, Lowell. *Cleon, Knights, and Aristophanes' Politics*. Lanham, Md.: University Press of America, 1987.

Edwards, Anthony. "Historicizing the Popular Grotesque: Bakhtin's Rabelais and His World and Attic Old Comedy." *Bakhtin and the Classics*. R. Bracht Branham, ed. Evanston, Ill.: Northwestern University Press, 2002.

Ehrenberg, Victor. *The People of Aristophanes: A Sociology of Old Attic Comedy*. 2nd ed. London: Methuen, 1874.

Elderkin, G. W. *Mystic Allusions in* The Frogs *of Aristophanes*. Princeton, N.J.: Princeton University Press, 1955.

Goldhill, Simon. *The Poet's Voice: Essays on Poetic and Greek Literature*. Cambridge: Cambridge University Press, 1991.

Gum, Coburn: *The Aristophanic Comedies of Ben Jonson*. The Hague: Mouton, 1969.

Holtermann, Martin. *Der deutsche Aristophanes: die Rezeption eines politischen Dichters in 19. Jahrhundert*. Göttingen, Germany: Vandenhoeck & Ruprecht, 2004.

Hornblower, Simon, and Antony Spawforth, eds. *The Oxford Classical Dictionary*. 3rd ed. Oxford: Oxford University Press, 1996.

Jernigan, Charlton. *Incongruity in Aristophanes*. Menasha, Wisc.: George Banta Publishing Company, 1939.

Konstan, D. *Greek Comedy and Ideology*. Oxford: Oxford University Press, 1995.

Kurten-Lindberg, Birgitta. *Women's Lib in Aristophanes' Athens?* Göteborg, Sweden: Astrom, 1987.

Moulton, Carroll. *Aristophanic Poetry*. Göttingen, Germany: Vandenhoeck & Ruprecht, 1981.

Murray, A. T. *On Parody and Paratragoedia in Aristophanes*. Berlin: Mayer & Müller, 1891.

Murray, Gilbert. *Aristophanes: A Study*. Oxford: Oxford University Press, 1933.

O'Regan, Daphne. *Rhetoric, Comedy, and the Violence of Language in Aristophanes'* Clouds. Oxford: Oxford University Press, 1992.

O'Sullivan, Neil. *Alcidimas, Aristophanes, and the Beginnings of Greek Stylistic Theory*. Stuttgart, Germany: F. Steiner, 1992.

Pelling, C. B. R. *Literary Texts and the Greek Historian*. London: Routledge, 2000.

Pickard-Cambridge, Arthur. *Dithyramb, Tragedy, and Comedy*. 2nd ed. Revised by T. B. L. Webster. Oxford: Oxford University Press, 1962.

Pütz, Babette. *The Symposium and Komos in Aristophanes*. Stuttgart: J. B. Metzler, 2003.

Rau, Peter. *Paratragödia: Untersuchung einer komischen Form des Aristophanes*. München: Beck, 1967.

Rosen, Ralph. *Old Comedy and the Iambographic Tradition*. Atlanta, Ga.: Scholars Press, 1988.

Segal, Erich, ed. *Oxford Readings in Aristophanes*. Oxford University Press, 1996.

Southard, Gretchen. *The Medical Language of Aristophanes*. Ann Arbor, Mich.: University Microfilms, 1971.

Strauss, Leo. *Socrates and Aristophanes*. Chicago: University of Chicago Press, 1980.

Sutton, Dana. *Self and Society in Aristophanes*. Washington, D.C.: University Press of America, 1980.

Taplin, Oliver. *Comic Angels and Other Approaches to Greek Drama Through Vase Paintings*. Oxford: Oxford University Press, 1993.

Van Steen, Gonda. *Venom in Verse: Aristophanes in Modern Greece*. Princeton, N.J.: Princeton University Press, 2000.

Vetter, Lisa. *Women's Work as Political Art: Weaving and Dialectical Politics in Homer, Aristophanes, and Plato*. Lanham, Md.: Lexington Books, 2005.

Willi, Andreas, ed. *The Languages of Aristophanes: Aspects of Linguistic Variation in Classical Attic Greek*. Oxford: Oxford University Press, 2003.

THEATERS, PRODUCERS

Hugill, William Meredith. *Panhellenism in Aristophanes*. Chicago: University of Chicago Press, 1936.

Keuls, Eva C. *The Reign of the Phallus: Sexual Politics in Ancient Athens*. Berkeley: University of California Press, 1985.

Murray, Gilbert. *Our Great War and the Great War of the Ancient Greeks*. New York: T. Seltzer, 1920.

Nichols, Peter. *Aristophanes' Novel Forms: The Political Role of Drama*. London: Minerva Press, 1998.

Robson, James. *Humour, Obscenity and Aristophanes*. Tübingen, Germany: Narr, 2006.

Rothwell, Kenneth. *Politics and Persuasion in Aristophanes'* Ecclesiazusae. New York: E. J. Brill, 1990.

_____. *Nature, Culture, and the Origins of Greek Comedy: A Study of Animal Choruses*. New York: Cambridge University Press, 2007.

Russo, Carlo. *Aristophanes, an Author for the State*. New York: Routledge, 1994.

Sandbach, F. *The Comic Theatre of Greece and Rome*. New York: Norton, 1977.

Sutton, Dana. *Ancient Comedy: The War of the Generations*. New York: Twayne Publishers, 1993.

Taaffe, Lauren. *Aristophanes and Women*. London: Routledge, 1993.

ACTORS, DIRECTORS, PROFESSIONALS

Cartledge, Paul. *Aristophanes and His Theatre of the Absurd*. Bristol, U.K.: Bristol Classical Press, 1999.

Collins, William. *Aristophanes*. Philadelphia: Lippincott, 1873.

Csapo, Eric, and William J. Slater. *The Context of Ancient Drama*. Ann Arbor: University of Michigan Press, 1994.

Deardon, C. W. *The Stage of Aristophanes*. London: University of London, Athlone Press, 1976.

Elliott, Richard. *Some Contributions to the Textual Criticism of Aristophanes and Aeschylus*. Oxford: Blackwell, 1908.

Fisher, Raymond. *Aristophanes'* Clouds: *Purpose and Technique*. Amsterdam: Hakkert, 1984.

Hubbard, Thomas. *The Masks of Comedy: Aristophanes and the Intertextual Parabasis*. Ithaca, N.Y.: Cornell University Press, 1991.

Lada-Richards, Ismene. *Initiating Dionysus: Ritual and Theatre in Aristophanes'* Frogs. New York: Oxford University Press, 1999.

Murray, Gilbert. *Aristophanes and the War Party: A Study of the Contemporary Criticism of the Peloponnesian War*. London: Allen and Unwin Ltd., 1919.

Parker, L. P. E. *The Songs of Aristophanes*. Oxford: The Clarendon Press, 1997.

Pickard-Cambridge, Arthur. *The Dramatic Festivals of Athens*. 2nd ed. Revised by J. Gould and D. M. Lewis. Oxford: Oxford University Press, 1968.

Platter, Charles. *Aristophanes and the Carnival of Genres*. Baltimore, Md.: Johns Hopkins University Press, 2007.

Revermann, Martin. *Comic Business: Theatricality, Dramatic Technique, and Performance Contexts of Aristophanic Comedy*. Oxford: Oxford University Press, 2006.

Richards, Herbert. *Aristophanes and Others*. London: G. Richards, 1909.

Schechter, Joel. *Satiric Impersonations: From Aristophanes to the Gorilla Girls*. Carbondale: Southern Illinois Press, 1994.

Segal, Erich. *The Death of Comedy*. Cambridge: Oxford University Press, 2001.

Sifakis, Gregory. *Parabasis and Animal Choruses*. London: Athlone Press, 1971.

Slater, Niall. *Spectator Politics: Metatheatre and Performance in Aristophanes*. Philadelphia: University of Pennsylvania Press, 2002.

Solomos, A. *The Living Aristophanes*. Ann Arbor: University of Michigan Press, 1974.

Spatz, Lois. *Aristophanes*. Boston: Twayne Publishers, 1978.

Stone, Laura. *Costume in Aristophanic Poetry*. Salem, N.H.: Ayer Co., 1984.

Ussher, Robert. *Aristophanes*. New York: Oxford University Press, 1979.

Vickers, Michael. *Pericles on Stage: Political Comedy in Aristophanes' Early Plays*. Austin: University of Texas Press, 1997.

Walcot, P. *Greek Drama in Its Theatrical and Social Context*. Cardiff: University of Wales Press, 1976.

While, John. *The "Stage" in Aristophanes*. Boston: Ginn & Company, 1891.

Whitman, Cedric. *Aristophanes and the Comic Hero*. Cambridge, Mass.: Harvard University Press, 1964.

Willi, Andreas, ed. *The Language of Greek Comedy*. Oxford: Oxford University Press, 2002.

EDITIONS OF ARISTOPHANES' WORK USED FOR THIS BOOK

Aristophanes. *The Complete Plays*. Vols. 1–3. Translated by Carl R. Mueller. Lyme, N.H.: Smith and Kraus, forthcoming.

SOURCES CITED IN THIS BOOK

Arnott, Peter. *Greek Scenic Conventions in the Fifth Century B.C.* Oxford: Oxford University Press, 1962.

Dover, Kenneth. "Greek Comedy." *Fifty Years (And Twelve) of Classical Scholarship*. 2nd ed. Maurice Platnauer, ed. Oxford: Blackwell, 1968.

_____. *Aristophanic Comedy*. Berkeley: University of California Press, 1972.

Henderson, Jeffrey, ed. *Aristophanes: Essays in Interpretation*. Cambridge: Cambridge University Press, 1980.

_____. "The *Demos* and Comic Competition." *Nothing to Do with Dionysos?* John J. Winkler and Froma I. Zeitlin, eds. Princeton, N.J.: Princeton University Press, 1989.

_____. *The Maculate Muse: Obscene Language in Attic Comedy*. 2nd ed. Oxford: Oxford University Press, 1991.

Jaeger, Werner. *Paideia: the Ideals of Greek Culture*. 3 vols. 2nd ed. New York: Oxford University Press, 1945.

MacDowell, Douglas M. *Aristophanes and Athens: An Introduction to the Plays*. Oxford: Oxford University Press, 1995.

McLeish, Kenneth. *The Theatre of Aristophanes*. London: Taplinger, 1980.

Sommerstein, A. H., ed. *Tragedy, Comedy and the Polis*. Bari, Italy: Levante Editori, 1993.

Whitman, Cedric. *The Heroic Paradox: Essays on Homer, Sophocles, and Aristophanes*. Ithaca, N.Y.: Cornell University Press, 1982.

Awards

"And the winner is . . ."

YEAR BC	DIONYSIA FESTIVAL IN ATHENS	LENAEA FESTIVAL IN ATHENS
427		Aristophanes *Banqueters* (second prize)
426	Aristophanes *Babylonians*	
425		Aristophanes *Acharnians*
424		Aristophanes *Knights*
423	Aristophanes *Clouds I* (third prize out of three)	
422		Aristophanes *Proagon* (first prize) Aristophanes *Wasps* (second prize)
421	Aristophanes *Peace I* (second prize)	
415	Xenocles *Oedipus, Lycaun, Bacchae, Athamas* (first prize) Euripides *Trojan Women, Alexandrus, Palamedes, Sisyphus* (second prize)	
414	Aristophanes *Birds* (second prize)	
410	Euripides *Phoenician Women* (second prize)	
409	Sophocles *Philoctetes*	
ca 405	Euripides *Bacchae* (posthumously produced)	Aristophanes *Frogs*
401	Sophocles *Oedipus at Colonus* (posthumously produced)	
387	Aristophanes *Cocolus*	

First prize unless otherwise specified

Aristophanes won prizes in the comedy genre; the others won in the tragedy genre.

INDEX

The entries in the index include highlights from the main In an Hour essay portion of the book.

ABOUT THE AUTHOR

Carl Mueller was a professor in the Department of Theater at the University of California, Los Angeles, from 1967 until his death in 2008. There he directed and taught theater history, criticism, dramatic literature, and playwriting. He was educated at Northwestern University, where he received a B.S. in English. After work in graduate English at the University of California, Berkeley, he received his M.A. in Playwriting at UCLA, where he also completed his Ph.D. in Theater History and Criticism. In 1960–1961 he was a Fulbright Scholar in Berlin.

A translator for more than forty years, he translated and published works by Büchner, Brecht, Wedekind, Hauptmann, Hofmannsthal, and Hebbel, to name a few. His published translation of von Horváth's *Tales from the Vienna Woods* was given its London West End premiere in July 1999. For Smith and Kraus he translated individual volumes of plays by Schnitzler, Strindberg, Pirandello, Kleist, and Wedekind. His translation of Goethe's *Faust* Part One and Part Two appeared in 2004. He also translated for Smith and Kraus *Sophokles: The Complete Plays* (2000), a two-volume *Aeschylus: The Complete Plays* (2002), and a four-volume *Euripides: The Complete Plays* (2005). His translations have been performed in every English-speaking country and have appeared on BBC-TV.

Smith and Kraus wishes to acknowledge Dr. Susan Ford Wiltshire, Professor of Classics, Emerita, Vanderbilt University. She was immensely helpful with the spellings of Greek names and places.

We thank Hugh Denard, whose enlightened permissions policy reflects an understanding that copyright law is intended to both protect the rights of creators of intellectual property as well as to encourage its use for the public good.

Know the playwright,
love the play.

Open a new door to theater study, performance, and audience satisfaction with these Playwrights In an Hour titles.

ANCIENT GREEK

Aeschylus   Aristophanes   Euripides   Sophocles

RENAISSANCE

William Shakespeare

MODERN

Anton Chekhov   Noël Coward   Lorraine Hansberry
Henrik Ibsen   Arthur Miller   Molière   Eugene O'Neill
Arthur Schnitzler   George Bernard Shaw   August Strindberg
Frank Wedekind   Oscar Wilde   Thornton Wilder
Tennessee Williams

CONTEMPORARY

Edward Albee   Alan Ayckbourn   Samuel Beckett
Theresa Rebeck   Sarah Ruhl   Sam Shepard   Tom Stoppard
August Wilson

To purchase or for more information
visit our web site inanhourbooks.com